ONLINE
SEDUCTIONS

ONLINE SEDUCTIONS

FALLING IN LOVE WITH STRANGERS ON THE INTERNET

ESTHER GWINNELL, M.D.

KODANSHA INTERNATIONAL
NEW YORK • TOKYO • LONDON

Kodansha America, Inc.
114 Fifth Avenue, New York, New York 10011, U.S.A.

Kodansha International Ltd.
17-14 Otowa 1-chome, Bunkyo-ku, Tokyo 112, Japan

Published in 1998 by Kodansha America, Inc.

Library of Congress Cataloging-in-Publication Data

Gwinnell, Esther.
Online seductions : falling in love with strangers on the Internet /
Esther Gwinnell.
p. cm.
Includes bibliographical references (p.   ) and Index.
ISBN 1-56836-214-5 (acid-free paper)
1. Dating (Social customs)—Computer network resources.   2. Man-
woman relationships—Computer network resources.   3. Love—
Computer network resources.   4. Internet (Computer network)   I.
Title.
HQ801.G95   1998
306.7'0285—dc21   97-50068

Book design by Gretchen Achilles
Manufactured in the United States of America on acid-free paper

98 99 00 01   10 9 8 7 6 5 4 3 2 1

WITH THANKS TO CHRISTINE ADAMEC FOR
HER TIRELESS HELP,

TO THE INHABITANTS OF THE INTERNET FOR
THEIR STORIES,

AND TO MY HUSBAND, MARC, FOR ALL THE REST.

CONTENTS

The participants in the e-mail vignettes in this book are composites. Their handles and biographical information have been invented, so that any resemblance to a real person is accidental.

The Internet consists of groups or networks of computers that span the globe, encompassing libraries of information and millions of participants. Nearly a million Americans connect with the Internet daily,[1] and globally more than 30 million people access the Internet every day. Some writers have talked about the Internet as a "cybersociety" in which residents shop, work, do research, write letters, make phone calls and "hang out" together at meeting places—as in a small town in the real world.

Although anyone with a computer and a modem can connect to the Internet directly, most people use an Internet connection service that provides e-mail capability, giving them access to the Internet without requiring an intimate knowledge of arcane computer commands. Attempts to organize and make accessible the enormous quantity of Internet information have been spotty but heroic—currently the major organizing factor is the World Wide Web, which indexes and coordinates Internet addresses to businesses, organizations and individuals all over the world.

One way of thinking about the Internet is to imagine it as an enormous convention center—with booths for every special interest, business, service and activity conceivable. There are booths (or Web sites) for skiing, fishing and science fiction, and discussion groups (or Usenet groups) for every color in the political spectrum, for medical information and support, fan clubs for rock stars and meeting areas for people seeking friendships and romances with other people of every description. At any given moment, live conversations involving from two to two hundred people are going on in "chat rooms" and on "chat boards."

Several large online services provide e-mail, internal library and reference materials and discussion groups for special interests, as well as chat boards. CompuServe, America Online, Prodigy and Microsoft Network are the primary such services. On CompuServe, I have participated in forums or discussion groups on such diverse subjects as travel to Morocco, mental health, the battle of the sexes and a multiplicity of political and current events. Many of the forums have "posted" messages, much like bulletin boards. In time, participants in the same forum or Usenet group recognize one another and form alliances and friendships. Shared interests can lead to more significant relationships, and even to deep attachments and love.

Over the past few years, my own experience in meeting people on the Internet has been varied. I have participated in various CompuServe discussion groups and chat boards and "surfed the Net" for information and entertainment. I have had extensive correspondence with people I have never met, and I have made friends on medical forums whom I later met at national medical meetings. I have formed friendships, some lasting years, with people I know only through the Internet, through writing and exchanging the latest jokes online. Friends and strangers have asked me for advice about troubling personal problems and about online romance, while even passing acquaintances aware that I am a psychiatrist have asked me about psychiatric medications and diagnoses. My own impression of Internet relationships is therefore fairly positive. I have met some interesting people and made a few good friends.

But when a good friend told me her husband was divorcing her because he had fallen in love with a woman he met on the Internet, I was stunned. It was unbelievable to me that such a thing could happen: that someone I knew could meet a total stranger on the Internet and form a relationship so intense that it would destroy an eight-year marriage.

In the course of the next few months, I had many discussions with people, both on the Internet and in my daily life, about this bizarre event—only to discover that many of them had also formed relationships with people they met on the Internet. In that period three of my psychotherapy patients reported forming intense relationships on the Internet, relationships that became a focus of their therapy sessions. Exploring why and how these relationships happen became my primary concern, both because of my patients and because of my own sadness about my friend's divorce.

Several patients began talking to me about their obsessive relationships online and about Internet addiction. Some were converting an obsessive behavior such as binge eating or shoplifting into an obsession with sex chat boards or with chat boards of any kind. The issue of Internet addiction began to be discussed in psychiatric circles—initially with humor, later with concern. At first, the focus of all these discussions was "Why is this happening?" Later, it became "What should we do about it?"

Little literature on the subject was available to me. The

only books I found were those that advised the reader *where* to find romantic or sexual connections on the Internet, giving scant attention to how and why these connections happen— and omitting warnings for readers to be careful. Discussions with friends and colleagues about falling in love on the Internet led to discussions with my own online correspondents about the same issue. It became clear to me that a book on this subject would be useful for many people, including those who are personally involved in computer relationships and those who are being hurt by computer relationships.

In writing this book, I have focused on trying to answer the two questions that seem to be the most important: Why is this happening? What should we do about it?

To begin to answer these questions, I decided to conduct an informal study among people on the Internet who had been involved in such an affair. I posted an invitation to participate in my research and a questionnaire on the newsgroup "alt.romance." In response, I received not only the completed questionnaires but also dozens of samples of romantic e-mail. (The e-mail messages that appear in this book are not ones that were actually sent between real online lovers; they represent, rather, a composite of many of the actual messages that were passed on to me.) With some of the respondents, I also conducted telephone interviews.

In addition, as a psychotherapist, I see many patients who are involved in online romances, and their stories have also contributed to this book. Finally, a number of correspondents have written to me for advice, knowing of my interest in and knowledge of online romances. I am grateful to all these people, whose participation made possible both my research and this book.

It can be as addictive as crack cocaine and as seductive as the strongest aphrodisiac. Yet, its effects can be so subtle that people don't even realize what's happening to them—until it's too late.

What is it? Love on the Internet. Today, men and women are meeting and falling in love with each other through CompuServe, America Online and any number of bulletin boards and services that crisscross both the United States and the world. It happens every day, involving individuals as far apart as New York and Helsinki.

Falling in love over a machine? Many people find the idea humorous or even ludicrous. Yet it is happening, and psychotherapy patients are reporting this phenomenon to mental health professionals worldwide. These romances present a puzzle for both the participants and for the therapeutic community. It has become important to explore the ways in which people fall in love on the Internet, and to understand the similarities and the differences between them and relationships formed in person.

The May 1996 issue of *Cosmopolitan* told the stories of a half-dozen electronic surfers who had met over the Internet and subsequently married. *Time* magazine reported in 1997 that divorces sparked by Internet affairs are becoming more and more common. The president of the American Academy of Matrimonial Lawyers says in this article, "I think it's going to be more and more of a big deal. People get into these chat rooms, and they start talking, and some of it gets really steamy."

In the July 1995 issue of *The Addiction Letter,* one psychiatrist says, "A lot of psychiatrists are not aware of how much time their patients are putting into e-mail relationships, committing e-mail adultery, getting involved with cyberspace S&M and just in general being obsessed."

Using electronic mail, private "chats" in "rooms" and even public discussion forums, men and women are meeting each other and becoming firmly attached to each other online. Some leave their spouses or significant others to pursue these exciting new people and form lasting attachments, while others give up their online loves and plummet into depression.

Romances with strangers are not an entirely new phenomenon. Since World War II, women have fallen in love with soldiers they met only through letters. Traditionally, letters written to soldiers or convicts have often resulted in the development of strong attachments. Many men and women have written to *Dear Abby,* thanking her for helping them meet the pen pal that they later married. In some ways today's computer communications are comparable to these letters. In both instances, the letter writers have no visual, aural or tactile cues, whether the person they are writing to is overseas in Bosnia or across the city.

It is difficult to say how many people fall in love with their computer pals, or how many become obsessed with Internet relationships. But it is clear that this phenomenon is widespread.

An estimated 8.4 million adults use the Internet, according to *The American Internet User Survey*. Internet usage has grown eightfold in just the last year, and the numbers will likely continue to climb. According to the *National Research Bureau* more than 30 million people worldwide access the Internet everyday. Even if only one percent of all of them is looking for love via their computers, that still totals nearly 300,000 adults. Even if the percentage is lower—say, half a percentage point—that still predicts that nearly 150,000 adults are becoming involved in intense computer relationships everyday.

The numbers seem astonishing. How can they be true? After all, we're just talking about typing notes on a computer, aren't we? Sending messages to strangers? But the fact is, electronic communication allows people to meet others online with whom they quickly, sometimes dangerously quickly, feel a close intimate connection. Because of the way people relate via computer, they can be deeply in love before they even notice what is happening.

When two people decide to communicate alone, either in a private chat room or via electronic mail, something can happen that cannot happen anywhere else in life. They give and receive no visual, aural or tactile cues. They smell no bad body odors, see no lettuce in the teeth that turns each other off; no intense gazes that scare each other away. No crow's-feet or laugh lines to remind each other of age. In fact, there are no reality-based signals to prevent the letter writers from having any fantasies they wish about each other.

With computer love, you can imagine anything you want about the other person's feelings. You can believe that the other person completely understands you and that you are sharing an emotional experience such as you have never had before. With the ease of communication and the opportunity to write out your thoughts, communicating online can feel like sharing the deepest and most hidden parts of yourself.

Of course, you cannot really read the other person's mind or know their feelings, but still the illusion persists. And because you have none of the usual cues to bring you back to reality, you may begin to attribute important qualities to the other person, especially idealistic and romantic qualities.

Computer relationships also offer anonymity, which can produce a sense of safety. You may share your most intimate thoughts and secrets with your computer partner, then find him also baring his soul to you. The anonymous somebody becomes a friend who truly understands you, somebody who *really* cares! Paradoxically, anonymity allows intense intimacy to develop in a very short time—like strangers on a train, people reveal their secrets, hopes and fears with little concern about the other person's opinion, at least initially.

While you may wish you could tell your husband about your lifelong dream of quitting work and sailing around the world, you may fear that he would laugh at you or even get angry. So you talk about this dream with an online friend instead. Just seeing these words on the screen, just writing about your hopes and dreams, intensifies their importance. At the same time it transfers great importance to the person you are writing to.

Good marriages have ended because of computer relationships, while others have been seriously damaged, hanging on by a thread. Many of us know people who are successfully married but who, for various reasons, are not communicating with their spouses. What we may not realize is that they may be communicating instead with their online friends. Some leave their marriage to pursue a relationship with someone they never met in person. Computer relationships have progressed from Internet intimacy to meetings in person and on to marriage. Many participants in computer relationships feel that their relationship is uniquely intimate—since it "grew from the inside out" instead of from the outside in, as face-to-face relationships do.

When Internet lovers leave the computer to go to other activities, they may feel as though the other person is "inside" them. As they go through their daily routine, they may be thinking of what to say to her or what she'll say later on. They may check repeatedly for messages throughout the day. It is not uncommon for people involved in a computer relationship to exchange dozens of messages every day.

As in ordinary relationships, though, some people in computer relationships take advantage of the other person. Some "court" more than one person online at once, juggling as many as three or four Internet romances. Sometimes they get caught because they use the same lines with everyone, and their correspondents compare notes. Some chat boards are specifically devoted to sexual conversation ("hot chat"), and the relationships formed there can be as shallow and sexual as any other one-night stand.

The lack of social and sensory cues also provides the opportunity for people to develop powerful fantasies about someone else online. These fantasies can lead to stalking, harassment and sometimes very real threats. Chat boards may be more likely to produce this kind of disturbed interaction because the participants are free to project their internal needs onto essentially invisible others. Once they get their needs met, they feel they know the person, even if the romance is happening only in their own fantasies.

Online Seductions is about how and why people form

romantic relationships online. Using composites of real-life examples, I will describe the psychological processes involved in Internet relationships. I'll tell you about some happy endings, but also about some of the more disturbed relationships. I'll give you some pointers on how to protect yourself online and how to deal with Internet relationships, and I'll offer some advice to therapists who are working with people caught up in Internet relationships.

Finally, if you want to contact me or chat about your own experiences, please visit my website (www.nocouch.com) or send me an e-mail (strangers@nocouch.com).

ONLINE
SEDUCTIONS

CHAPTER 1

Strangers in Love

LETTERS TO SOLDIERS

Before the Internet, there was the postal service. People have fallen in love in every conceivable situation, and some people who never met in person have fallen in love through the exchange of letters. This is what happened between Annie and Corporal Tom, a soldier stationed in Vietnam in 1967.

February 3, 1967

Dear Annie,
Sorry to be so long about writing back to you. Since your last letter, we have been slogging around in the jungle, and I haven't had any way to write to you. The VC have been busy this week, gearing up for the usual Tet (that means "spring") offensive, and that has kept us on our toes. It's been raining nearly continuously, warm rain, the kind of rain that rots out

your boots. Everybody here has some kind of foot fungus to go along with the constant dampness.

Since I got your picture, I like to think about you standing in your garden. I like to think about your garden, too. I've been in this country so long that I find myself thinking of home and gardens like yours the same way I think about movies or books I've read. They don't seem quite real to me, but you seem real to me. Looking at you in the picture makes you seem more real than anything else around here. I can almost smell the roses.

Is that a fruit tree behind you? Please tell me it's a peach tree! I know I have already complained to you about the food, but that is the soldier's complaint. Food is rarely even what I used to consider edible, and some nights in the bunker, when I have one ear cocked for unusual noises, I drift into dreams about (don't laugh, now) peaches. Rich, luscious peaches still warm from the sun, the smell of them, the feel of the peach fuzz on my teeth.

I've been carrying your picture in my chest pocket, you know, the place where guys carry their Bibles in hopes of stopping that stray shot. Only now I've got you there, and I look at you a lot, trying to remind myself that home is real and that I am really going to get there again. I like to think about going to the drive-in with you, and eating hamburgers and drinking Coca-Cola delivered by carhops, and the ground would be dry and my feet would be dry. When I get home, can I take you to the drive-in?

Sorry about the condition of this letter. I haven't got much paper available right now, and this is the worse for the wear. I'll try to find something better next time.

You know I can't wait to hear from you again, my home girl. Send me another piece of home soon (I know you can't send me a peach!).

Always yours,
Corporal Tom

(This letter, stained and wrinkled, received March 5, 1967)

Some four months after he sent this letter, Corporal Tom was wounded in Vietnam and was medically evacuated to the States. Annie met him at the airport, and later they went to that drive-in movie together. They married in the fall of 1968 and have celebrated more than twenty-five years of marriage. Sometimes, on a warm summer night when the peaches are ripe, they sit under the trees and talk about the letters they wrote, the letters that drew them together and how they fell in love long before they ever met in person.

During the Korean War and the Vietnam War, thousands of strangers met and corresponded through letters like these—then fell in love. *Dear Abby* has printed many letters from people who met through Operation Dear Abby, a letter drive for soldiers. The stories of their romances are often poignant and sometimes funny, but always two people fell in love who were strangers to each other—strangers they knew only through the written word.

For Operation Dear Abby, schoolchildren wrote letters and young women wrote letters. The USO amassed barrels of these letters and generally divided them by state of origin, so that the soldiers could choose letters from their home state.

Sometimes those letters formed the basis for a relationship that resulted in love and marriage. One man told me of picking up a letter from a barrel that had been wrongly filed—and answering it anyway. He later met the woman who wrote it, and they were married.

For soldiers, living in a world of danger, jungles and booby traps, these letters provided a remembrance of home, a sense of connection to ordinary life. The intensity of their yearning for ordinary life fueled the importance they attached to the letters, and in the jungles and the mountains, under combat conditions, they wrote their own letters back to the unknown women.

Like Corporal Tom, many thought almost constantly about the letters and the letter writer, daydreaming about what they would do when they went home. They daydreamed of sitting under peach trees or going to a drive-in, sitting next to the woman. The daydreams fostered a still-greater sense of attachment, and the letter writer became a symbol for home, for that place in their daydreams where home existed.

Falling in love through letters is far different from falling in love face to face. With the letters to the soldiers, usually no face was attached to the writer; a soldier had no real information about who she was or what she looked like (unless she sent a photograph). In normal peacetime many of the writers would never have met in person. Their sense of shared common interests and common experiences came from the letters themselves.

A powerful sense of romance can spring from writing letters to someone you don't know and whose life is very different from yours. The idea of writing to a soldier, whose life is in constant danger, lends a fairy-tale quality to the writing. The strength of this feeling can make each letter valuable, even treasured. The woman's fear for the safety of the soldier, his longing for home, and their common daydreams about some future time of safety and even joy all combined to make these letters important in a way that took them out of the realm of the ordinary.

NOT ENTIRELY STRANGERS

Even from these almost-anonymous letters, the letter writers can learn many things about each other. For his part, the most obvious fact about him is that he is a soldier, in a foreign land. His name and rank can be found in his return address; he is likely to be between the ages of eighteen and twenty-five, and his situation can be imagined from news reports and from the physical condition of the letter pages.

The young woman writing these letters also supplies information about herself, often information she has no idea she is conveying. For example, she may write on humorous stationery or perfume her envelopes. She may use elegant paper, or she may write on notebook paper. Her ethnic heritage may be inferred from her name, and clues to her education and intellect may be found in her handwriting and spelling.

Especially under adverse conditions, the character of the writers becomes evident. As Marsha remembers, "I knew Jeff was in combat a lot, and that the conditions were terrible. I don't know how he wrote to me so much. He must have spent every spare minute writing those letters—some of them were ten pages long, written very small and on both sides of the page. But you know, every letter he wrote had jokes in it, jokes that were going around or funny things he thought of to say about the guys in his unit, about the food or about the people in the villages.

"I thought to myself, here's this guy in the jungle somewhere, thinking of me. Here he is, every day hard and dangerous, and he still makes jokes! I think I fell in love with him for making jokes when everything around him was so awful. A guy like that, you know that he isn't going to be thrown by anything life hands him."

Marsha believed that she learned more about Jeff from those letters than she would have if she had first met him in person. When they did meet, he was very shy and quiet, and it took several dates before his shyness wore off enough for her to see the Jeff she knew from the letters. She knows that if she hadn't already known from his letters that the humor and strength were in there somewhere, she would never have had a second date with him. Now, every anniversary, their children happily tell the story of how Mom and Dad met through letters during the war.

Not all of the soldiers' stories have a fairy-tale ending. Some of their marriages ended after a few years, while others couldn't make the connection in person that they had made on paper. For a few of the soldiers, their feelings of love, formed under combat conditions, didn't survive the transition to coming home and reconnecting with their life before the war. Yet while they were in Korea or Vietnam, these soldiers had felt themselves to be deeply in love with their pen pals and spent their days and nights dreaming of the time when they would be together.

WHY STRANGERS FALL IN LOVE

Several factors contributed to the development of loving relationships between the writers of these letters. One, as already noted, was the sense of importance that these letters had to the writers. They were not ordinary business correspondence, or casual letters between friends. They were letters between The War and Home, letters from danger to safety, letters that seemed to form a lifeline between two people. Those who maintained the correspondence invested their emotions in it: even if no romance was involved, they made a commitment to continue it.

Another factor is that many of the soldiers and the women were single. They were likely close in age, and both had already made some effort to reach out. This increased the likelihood that they were at least theoretically available for a relationship. Some soldiers corresponded with several writers, and some of the women wrote letters to several soldiers. The situation was ripe for romantic relationships to develop between the authors of these letters.

Finally, there is a magic to the written word. Receiving letters has a mystique that is just not available in face-to-face relationships. If you look in your closet, chances are that you have a small (or large!) bundle of love letters from some period in your life, tied with a ribbon and carefully preserved. The words may be pretty mundane, and the lover may long since have left your life, but you can recall the memory of love from those letters in a way that other forms of communication cannot duplicate.

With all these factors combined, it is hardly surprising that letter writers became very attached to each other. But we are still left with the question of how these men and women *fell in love* with strangers, people whom they had never met before, whom they did not see or touch or smell. These strangers had never spoken to each other on the phone and would not have recognized each other if they met on the street.

Corporal Tom's letter shows us some of the reasons he made that romantic connection with Annie. He daydreamed about her, and she filled his thoughts whenever he needed something pleasant to think about. He could have fantasies about her, filling in the gaps in his information about who she was in real life with the qualities of his own ideal woman. She would love dancing maybe, or she would really enjoy swimming at that beach he always went to when he was sixteen. He invested his fantasy life in Annie, and she became for him an ideal woman because whatever he didn't know about her—what she was like, how she moved, what her voice sounded like—he could invent from his own daydreams.

Tom also built fantasies of a future with Annie as a way of avoiding thinking about his current situation. In this way he reassured himself that he would actually have a future, that he would someday get out of "this stinking jungle" and go back home to drive-in movies and peaches and a girl in a long dress in a garden.

Certainly, as they exchanged letters, he modified his ideas about her. Annie actually didn't swim, but she did like dancing; she had cut her hair, and it was different from the picture. She was really into baking and was more of a homebody than he had imagined. But until they met in person, there would always be gaps in his knowledge of her.

For her part, Annie made up a picture of Tom based on television news reports showing soldiers in Vietnam. She originally had thought of him simply in uniform, like the soldiers she saw at a military base near her home. But the television pictures of soldiers were different; they were dirty and tired and their uniforms looked different—they were wearing camouflage or seemed to be only partly wearing uniforms. They looked hot and hadn't shaved. She saw one soldier that she thought of as being like Tom, and whenever she thought of Tom, it was this television image that she saw in her mind.

Both Tom and Annie were willing to feel deeply about each other without meeting. As they wrote to each other, they shared thoughts they had never shared with anyone else before. Annie wrote about her feelings about the war, and her sense of being a part of a bigger world than she had previously experienced, because a part of her was now connected to this soldier in Vietnam. Tom wrote about his experiences, and his sense of how he was changing because of those experiences. The process of writing to this stranger was deepening his introspection, increasing his self-understanding in a way that was not possible anywhere else in his danger-filled life.

Using the letter writing as a form of diary keeping, Annie told Tom about her daily activities: about running into friends at the market, the movies she saw, the books she read, an argument she had with her mother. All were gratefully received. Although she wrote the letters for Tom, they also served her as a place to pause in her day and think about her world. In this sense, the letters served a therapeutic need for them both.

By itself, this kind of intimacy would have increased the sense of connection between them. But the warmth of their letters and their mutual feeling of being listened to increased their intimacy, until they both felt that they were sharing from the soul. Letting down the barriers for intimacy lets down the barriers for caring and attachment; sharing secrets creates a bond. That bond, plus the daydreams and the magic of letters, led Annie and Tom to fall in love.

Their facelessness to each other actually contributed to the intimacy of the writing. Because no relationship had existed before, there was little risk for either Tom or Annie in being honest and open. They would not be running into each other at parties or at the grocery store. They would not be dealing in person with the real human being to whom they were writing. They could be as intimate with each other as they wanted and needed to be.

Annie, who wrote as though she were writing in her diary, had a sense that Tom was somehow an extension of herself. He would not be truly real to her until she met him in person. Until that time, she created an image of him based both on the information in his letters and on her own imagination.

Some famous diary keepers have also created an image of the person they were writing to. When Anne Frank wrote in her diary, she created a fictional character to write to, so that she could imagine an emotional connection between herself and "Kitty," her reader. Although Tom was certainly more real to Annie than Kitty was to Anne Frank, he was still essentially without form until their actual physical meeting.

This is not to suggest that the love that Annie and Tom felt for each other was anything less than deep, intense and abiding. Had Tom been killed in combat instead of wounded, Annie would have grieved for his loss even if they never met, as she would have for anyone else she loved. But that grief would also have been different from her grief for someone she knew and loved in person.

TANGIBLE EVIDENCE OF LOVE

When I was in medical school and my then-boyfriend was in law school in another state, I waited for his letters with an eagerness that is hard to describe. Letters can be read again and again and be savored and cherished in a way that phone calls cannot. I could write to him in the middle of the night (and often did), and I could reread his letters for comfort or company whenever I wanted.

It wasn't that his letters were masterpieces of the written word, or filled with poetry. They were just discussions of the day's activities, written in his own handwriting and carrying with them the flavor of who he was. But they were tangible proof of his existence—I could touch them and see them and read them when I was lonely. Every trip to the mailbox made me slightly anxious: Would there be a letter today? Or would I have to wait until tomorrow? I would hope for a really long letter, because it would take longer to read, and it would mean he had spent a lot of time writing it and thinking about me. The joy of finding a letter, or the disappointment of going away empty-handed—each day held the possibility of either outcome.

Being far from home and under a fair amount of stress, I would deeply appreciate every letter. I engaged in a lively correspondence with many friends from college, and it was a rare day that I had no mail at all. As special as the letters from my boyfriend were, all the letters I got from my friends were important, too.

PEN-PAL ROMANCES

Another way that people have met through letters alone is
through having a pen pal. A fairly common activity for
schoolchildren, writing to a pen pal is also popular among
young adults who enjoy writing letters. A bit of a fantasy is
always involved in writing to a pen pal, especially the fantasy
that you will make a lifelong friend, preferably in some
romantic and faraway place. (And of course, wherever *you*
are will seem romantic and faraway to your pen pal.)

The method by which pen pals connect is similar to that
of soldiers and the women back home. Generally, both writers are interested in having a pen pal. Among young people,
the likelihood is greater that the pen pals will be of the same
gender, if only because people who get pen pals seem predis-
posed to finding someone as like themselves as possible.
Women tend to write to women, and more women (or girls)
seem to want pen pals than men. But if they are of the right
age and gender, pen pals can also fall in love.

Branwyn was fifteen years old and living in Ireland when
she got a letter at school from a boy in New York whose class
was doing a project on Irish history. Patrick was sixteen and
of Irish heritage. He'd sent his letter to the mayor of the town
his family came from, asking that it be forwarded to someone
in the school who would be willing to help him. Branwyn collected stamps, so she ended up with the task of answering the
letter in exchange for obtaining the stamps from it.

Over the next few years, Branwyn and Patrick wrote to
each other a few times a month. Patrick would send her
stamps that he collected just for her, and he would tell her
about his day-to-day struggles with science classes and his

dashed hopes of making first string on the football team. Quite a lively exchange occurred when it became clear to both of them that football meant something quite different to an Irish girl and an American boy.

There never seemed to be much likelihood that they would meet; their families were not wealthy, and neither had ever traveled outside their own country. But the letters continued, and the two became good friends. They sent each other their school pictures. Branwyn continued on to the university to study biology, and Patrick went on to take a job with an airline. Suddenly the possibility of meeting moved from daydream to reality. After four years of corresponding, they suddenly became aware of each other not just as good but long-distance friends, but also as possible lovers.

Branwyn dug out her old pictures of Patrick and reminded herself of his growth from boy to man. As they wrote back and forth sharing their fears and hopes about a possible meeting, their letters intensified in their emotional content. Some time had to pass before Patrick had put enough time in with the airline to fly to Ireland, which meant they had lots of time to get cold feet, to get panicked and to reassure themselves that they had been friends for years. Even if no relationship came out of the meeting, they could still have a good visit, and Branwyn would have a chance to show Patrick around his ancestral home.

Patrick, on his end, was looking daily at Branwyn's photograph. He found himself entranced with thoughts of her. He reread all her letters and laughed at the childish things they had once written. But when he finally came to Ireland, he was disconcerted to find that he had a hard time understanding what she was saying, while she was taken aback by how tall he was. These differences between fantasy and reality were initially very difficult for both of them to deal with. But after only a few days Patrick was just as entranced with the real Branwyn as he had been with his pen pal.

On his second visit to Ireland, Patrick proposed marriage, and Branwyn accepted. With their parents' help, Branwyn transferred to a university in New York, and Patrick and Branwyn later married.

The relationship between Patrick and Branwyn has some features that are different from the soldiers' relationships with women back home. Obviously, neither one was in danger, and they were engaged in writing to each other as teenagers. In a sense, they grew up together. They never expected to be able to meet, and so their fantasies about each other were not "rehearsals" for a meeting. That lack of a possibility for meeting also freed them from restrictions on what they might say to each other.

In adolescence, many young people are driven to try to be "normal" or like the other teens around them. They hide their inner selves from one another, carefully watching to see whether their own feelings match those of the teens around them, fearing exposure as being "different," even while striving in some sense to be unique. For Patrick and Branwyn, this tendency to hide from each other's scorn was reduced (though not absent) because they never thought they would really meet.

Still, their interaction had a romantic quality because they lived in different countries and were boy and girl—this is the stuff that movies are made of. The length of their correspondence is quite remarkable, and few of the Internet couples who responded to my questionnaire even came close to writing for five years before meeting. In the course of this correspondence, Branwyn and Patrick had essentially gone to school together and grown up together.

Both had daydreamed about the person they were writing to. Each created a mental image, one that incorporated information from the letters but that was also heavily based on books and movies about the other's country. When Patrick watched movies about Ireland, he thought of Branwyn. When Branwyn read books about America, she thought of Patrick. Over the years their exchange of photographs allowed them to visualize each other, but their ideas about how the other would talk, behave and even dress in real life were all fantasy.

Like the soldiers and their female pen pals, Patrick and Branwyn developed a degree of intimacy that was greater than the intimacy of any of their relationships in their day-to-day life. Fortunately for them, they were able to transfer that intimacy from letters to a face-to-face relationship. This does not always happen. The differences between daydream and reality can create a tremendous barrier between two people, even people who have already shared a great deal about themselves in writing. For an international couple like Patrick and Branwyn, the difference in their two cultures might have enhanced those barriers to the point that they would be uncomfortable with each other in person, even though writing back and forth had been easy.

PRISON PEN PALS

Finally, there is another group of pen pals: people who correspond with convicts in the penitentiary. Frequently men, and occasionally women, who are incarcerated advertise for a pen pal in personal columns and student newspapers. From this correspondence, just as with the other kinds, people have fallen in love with and even married while the convict was still incarcerated. (Because of the prevalence of women on the "outside" writing to men on the "inside," I will discuss these relationships in terms of women falling in love with male convicts. But that doesn't mean that men have not met and fallen in love with women who are in prison.)

Joe, with help from a friend on the outside, put an ad in the campus weekly newspaper in a midwestern college town. The ad read "25 year old man in prison seeks pen pal. Strong Christian beliefs, interest in current books. Write to . . ."

Laurie, a twenty-year-old transfer student at the college, was tired of going to her mailbox and finding it empty. So although doing so made her somewhat anxious, she sent a letter to Joe after she saw his ad. She reassured herself that he was in prison and even if he turned out to be weird or scary, she would be safe. Laurie felt a little proud of herself for doing something that her friends thought was brave (although they might also have said foolhardy). Joe wrote back to her almost immediately, a very warm and friendly letter, with references to the Bible study he was doing and the books he was reading in prison.

Although Laurie was a little uncomfortable with the immediate warmth of his response, she comforted herself with the Bible references and told herself that Joe must have been "born again" in prison and was probably a better person because of it. In later letters, he told her that he had been wrongly accused and that he had never committed the armed robbery of which he was convicted. They wrote back and forth about books and about religion, and Joe's letters to Laurie became quite romantic. He rhapsodized about her kindness in writing to him, about her intelligence and about her warm heart, and he complimented her frequently on her insight and understanding of the world around her.

After a few months of writing, Joe sent a letter that said that he wouldn't be able to write so often anymore because he didn't have money for stamps or paper. Laurie immediately sent him five dollars and a packet of stamps. She was invested in continuing the correspondence; she was getting attached to Joe and the image of herself she saw through his writing. She wanted to continue to feel as wonderful as Joe's letters made her feel.

Probably most people reading this vignette can predict the outcome of this relationship. If it had been happening to a friend, even Laurie could have predicted it. But because she was deeply involved, and because she had persuaded herself that the relationship was safe, she was not paying attention to the warning signs. She had accepted Joe's explanation for why he was in prison without considering that he might be deceiving her. She continued to accept that he was telling the truth without asking anyone around her for advice or information.

Laurie didn't tell her friends about her correspondence with Joe. In fact, she treasured the secret quality of their relationship. The secrecy allowed her to have fantasies about him without involving her friends, who might say negative things about the relationship. It allowed her to obsess about the letters and about Joe without permitting reality to modify her fantasies.

In fact, she had a sense that she was doing something illicit. This slight feeling of rebellion and a touch of danger heightened her emotions around every letter. The secrecy intensified her warm feelings toward Joe and accelerated her attachment to him.

Someone once said that one can identify a true sociopath in this way: If his female lawyer falls in love with him, then he's a sociopath. Because the art of deception is so ingrained in the most criminal among us, sociopaths seem to have a talent for finding the weak spots in the people around them and for playing to those weak spots. Laurie was lonely and insecure about her intelligence. She didn't like the way she looked, and she felt that no one would ever really love her. So when Joe began to compliment those exact things, to encourage her to believe that he was falling in love with her, she became deeply attached to him.

In the face of clear information that he was a convicted felon, this tangle of emotions led Laurie to become very attached to Joe. It may be difficult to understand relationships between women and prisoners, and it can seem absurd that a woman would marry a convict while he was still in prison, their relationship based only on writing letters. But the slight sense of rebellion and danger, combined with the heightened emotions of the writer and the construction of fantasies, all lead to the possibility of the woman forming a deep emotional attachment. The fact that the attachment may be unwise is usually not enough to prevent a susceptible woman from falling in love with a prisoner.

FROM THE POST OFFICE TO THE INTERNET

Communication on the Internet is just as likely to turn up dangerous or deceptive people as any other interaction with strangers. Although prisons are not yet online, con artists and social deviants of all kinds have the same access to computers and modems as good and honest people, which makes romantic connections on the Internet as risky as any social interaction with strangers. The perceived safety in letter writing is amplified on the computer and may even be *too* great, promoting unwise relationships.

For one thing, the diary-keeping experience of letter writing is even more intense over the Internet. Writing e-mail is easy enough that it relieves the writer of distractions that might otherwise inhibit communication. No search for paper or stamp is necessary, and the adept typist can write nearly as rapidly as he can think. The basic feeling of writing out one's thoughts to a faceless other person is common to both computer relationships and letters written to unknown soldiers.

Many teenagers who would once have formed relationships with teenagers in other countries as pen pals now meet their peers online. With the Internet, it is easy to write a note to a friend in England or Australia and to correspond with other young people throughout the world. Writing to someone living in another country has the same attraction over the Internet as in pen-pal correspondence, and e-mail provides the same sense of safety from peer judgment, enhanced by the ease of connecting.

But the differences between Internet relationships and ordinary letter-writing relationships are also important. Much of the nonverbal information that can be gleaned from letters is not available in Internet communication. There is no handwriting, no stationery, no dependable return address and sometimes no real name to convey clues about the real person. Internet relationships begin with even more anonymity, and they progress without the social and personal clues that an ordinary letter would provide.

These similarities and differences between Internet relationships and other anonymous relationships are worth noting because the newness of Internet relationships may make them seem abnormal or strange. Yet in letters to soldiers, pen pals and prisoners, we find the basic components of Internet relationships.

CHAPTER 2

The Intimacy of Online Communication

COUPLE SEAL INTERNET COURTSHIP IN TIMES SQUARE

NEW YORK—It was "love at first byte" for a couple who met on the Internet and sealed their romance Wednesday by exchanging wedding vows beamed onto a 100-foot E-mail bulletin board in Times Square.

Bob Norris and Catherine Smylie of Columbia, South Carolina, met online in an Internet chatroom last August, began a courtship in cyberspace and then agreed to meet after a month of heavy typing.

To cap it all, Norris proposed to Smylie over the Internet on an E-mail underwear billboard in Times Square, and that is where they were married Wednesday amid sunshine, noisy traffic and joined by parents, friends and a cluster of curious onlookers.

"The wedding not only represents the times we live in, but that Bob and Catie are confident and close enough to be here today speaks volumes about the future of this partnership," said Nicholas Graham, chief underwear officer for Joe Boxer, the company whose billboard transmits E-mail messages in the heart of New York City.

Mayor Rudolph Giuliani officiated in what was billed as the world's first digital wedding as Norris, 34, and Smylie, 27, read their vows to each other as they were transmitted on the electronic billboard and over the Internet.

In some respects the wedding was traditional, with the bride dressed in glimmering white and the groom in a tuxedo. They were going on to honeymoon in Europe.

Almost a dozen couples have proposed via the 100-foot-long message strip attached to the lower half of a 6,000-square-foot advertising billboard in Times Square, which was described by the underwear company as the world's largest.

REUTERS

It may be that in our industrialized, nuclear family culture, we have grown to crave intimacy. The increased distance between work and family life and the increased isolation of the working family have decreased our options for connectedness. Long work weeks, "cocooning," coming home after work to spend the evening watching television—all have taken their toll on the complexity of human networks.

When our workday lasts into the evening, we have fewer opportunities for idle conversation, either with family members or with people outside the family. Our free time is divided between seeing to essential responsibilities and watching television or doing very focused activities like skiing or sailing. Contact outside the family becomes more limited. Yet for the most part, within marriages and within nuclear families, intimacy needs are not adequately met.

Once we are out of school, our network of friends and our opportunities for developing new and varied relationships decrease markedly—with two very noticeable effects. One, the decreased opportunities make it harder for us to meet our needs for intimacy. Even idle conversation is greatly curtailed, and since sharing important thoughts or exploring daydreams and fantasies can happen only during long, rambling conversations that have no particular time limit, there's an additional loss of chances for intimacy.

Two, for those who are not in a committed romantic relationship, it becomes more difficult to make emotional connections. In part because adults have fewer opportunities to meet new people, the use of personal ads in newspapers has flourished, and on the Internet sites for personal ads and romantic connections are widespread. Dating services have become commonplace. The workplace has some serious limitations in terms of forming romantic relationships, and some workplaces are further limited by the number and gender of one's co-workers.

It is clear that for many people Internet relationships can provide experiences of intimate communication, intimate connections that are not available in face-to-face interactions in daily life. To some degree it's simply a matter of numbers—as millions of people take to the Internet, joining online services and sending messages, their opportunities to get to know one another increase exponentially. No other place, outside school, allows so many people to meet on common ground. With *mil-*

lions of people leaving notes for each other in cyberspace, friends (and enemies) are made. Some people find love, some find sex and some find the intellectual stimulation they haven't had since midnight conversations in the campus coffee shop.

FROM STRANGERS TO LOVERS

Some people online are actively seeking a person to date, while others are looking for friendship. Even those who are just trying to get needed or interesting information about a hobby or a problem may find much more than they expected—unsought love with a stranger.

The innocent quality of the first contact often leads to some of the dilemmas typical of computer romance. Getting involved in an interesting debate or political discussion, investigating a common problem or even uniting against a common "enemy" in a flame war can lead to a sense of unity and closeness that takes both parties by surprise.

The sense of commonality and relationships that develop in this way generally follow a similar course (although it will vary from couple to couple).

1. **Casual communication begins.**

2. **One person expresses interest in what another has said.**

3. **The two send public messages to each other.**

4. **These lead to private messages and chats.**

5. **The messages become more personal, longer and more involved.**

6. **One person begins to use a term of endearment like**

"dear" or "sweetie," or a physical sign-off such as "Big hugs." The other person follows this lead.

7. The messages become more frequent.

8. The couple speak on the phone.

9. They exchange photos.

10. They decide to meet.

At this point, the relationship either continues or comes to an end.

A computer relationship can thus start out casually, as one person responds to a message posted on a forum or Usenet group, where it is available for all to see. People with common interests naturally congregate in certain groups, and as they post messages, they may find that they share even more issues, hobbies or beliefs. Within even these public messages, many interpersonal and personality cues are available. For example, you may see a particularly intriguing message that you strongly agree with, then find yourself typing off a positive letter to that person.

You may post a message yourself about an issue or problem and receive a very sympathetic and helpful response from someone who seems to really understand you. Or you may respond with sympathy to the pain in someone else's message, or with delight to a humorous comment. These sympathetic and understanding responses, these appreciative and approving interactions, are deeply gratifying. During the course of your day, they may be the only gratifying responses you receive, the only times when someone "really sees" your wit, your thoughtfulness or your inner pain. You begin to exchange private e-mails with this person.

As the relationship intensifies, the frequency of the communication may increase to daily or even several times per day. People with continuous computer access, say, at an office, may send and receive dozens of postings every day. Checking your e-mail box becomes exciting and interesting. The more messages you send and receive, the more often you feel hope and then pleasure. Your fantasies about the other person intensify and become more important to your emotional life. For some, sexual writing and "computer sex" quickly become a part of the interaction, while for others, only romantic longings are evident.

Because the online communication gives no cues other than actual words, you'll both eventually want to hear what the other actually sounds like. So as the relationship intensifies, you may try talking on the phone.

If the phone conversation feels positive, sooner or later most online couples will want to either meet or exchange photos. You may scan a photo of yourself into a computer file and send it over the computer. Or you may send pictures through "snail mail" (the postal service). Even as phone conversations become more frequent, however, the frequency and intensity of the e-mail also increases. Some couples may spend as many as six to ten hours *a day* writing to, talking to and reading e-mail from each other.

CLUES TO WHAT A PERSON IS *REALLY* LIKE

With so few real-world cues, how can e-mail relationships become so intimate? How, in this medium, can strangers meet and form attachments powerful enough to lead to marriage— or divorce?

We are accustomed to gathering a great deal more nonverbal information from people we meet in person. Within *minutes* of arriving at a social gathering, most people find someone else in attendance to be either appealing or repellent, based on myriad tiny pieces of information that may never even reach the person's consciousness. Later they may ask themselves, "How did I manage to pick the one person in that group who was the most like my old boyfriend?" or "How did I zero in on the one person in the room who was an alcoholic," was a drug addict or had tremendous dependence problems, or who was narcissistic or had problems with intimacy?

On a day-to-day basis, we meet people and *immediately* form conclusions about their likely personality style and philosophy based on their clothing. In the 1970s John T. Malloy wrote a book called *Dress for Success,* in which he explored the ways in which people form judgments based on clothing. People imagine, he found, that men in dark blue suits are more trustworthy than those wearing brown suits. In *The Woman's Dress for Success Book,* he shows that a woman's clothing also inspires beliefs about what she is "really" like. Malloy's idea is that people can have a significant impact on how they are viewed in the world by choosing their clothing carefully.

A man with long hair and a beard, wearing a Grateful Dead T-shirt and Birkenstock shoes, conveys something about himself and his life that an observer instantly grasps—and the observer makes choices based on what he or she grasps. An observer who is generally attracted to people who are living unconventional lives outside the mainstream may be attracted to such a man.

A woman who is wearing a severely cut suit, with her hair pulled back and carefully chosen accessories, may convey that she lives in the business world. Her clothing suggests that she possesses ambition and the other personality traits associated with a business career. If you are attracted to ambitious or "strong" women, this woman will catch your eye, even in a crowd.

Other characteristics of physical appearance—weight, height, beauty—are all prominently obvious and immediately visible. Sometimes people rely on such clues to avoid the kinds of relationships that they have learned are recipes for disaster. Sarah reported to me that in social situations she watches now for evidence of heavy drinking because that is the only way she can avoid forming intense relationships with heavy drinkers. Within minutes of meeting someone at a social gathering, she forms a conclusion and either moves on or stays to talk. Fred, for his part, says that he has become very aware of women who are "too vivacious" because they are not only attractive to him but also destructive. Several relationships with such women have been disasters for him, storm-filled love affairs that left him depressed and angry.

My friend Jane tells me that she avoids men wearing Birkenstocks because they are "too laid back," by which she means they don't have strong financial ambitions to match her own. Pam tells me she won't date a man whose clothes don't fit right—she has decided from her experience that this means she will be the "caretaker" in the relationship. She has had a series of relationships with passive and dependent men who don't take care of themselves and rely on her to do it for them. People make such assessments blindingly fast, and for Jane, Sarah and Fred, they have become tremendously important.

In contrast, the computer screen provides little in the way of personal information. When someone writes to us on the Internet, we can't see their shoes, we can't smell their breath, body odor or perfume, and we can't make our usual judgments for or against that person. We cannot even assume that the writer owns a computer, since many coffeehouses and even public libraries provide Internet access. Poor spelling does not necessarily mean lower educational status—it may just convey poor typing skills, or the lack of a dependable spell-checker. No fragrance, no stationery, no handwriting are present to convey other clues—the typing on a computer screen is as uniform and anonymous as it can be.

One anonymous e-mail correspondent reported in dismay that after spending much time writing e-mail back and forth and talking on the phone, she decided to meet with her e-mail lover. He walked off the plane "looking like he hadn't washed his clothes in a month and had never even *looked* at a toothbrush."[1]

The use of "handles," or abbreviated names in Internet addresses, strips away even a person's name, which might otherwise tell us about their ethnic heritage or gender. Certainly some information is available in the handles people choose for themselves. On some of the more heavily used services, like America Online or Prodigy, many handles are frequently requested or are already being used. The handles that people are then assigned can be meaningless jumbles of words and numbers, or they can be very far from what an individual would have chosen for themselves. Until very recently, CompuServe has used numbers exclusively.

On some chat boards with significant sexual content, handles have more to do with drawing attention than with self-expression. Since many handles either mislead about or conceal gender or sexual preference, attempts to form conclusions based on them can be very mistaken. Some people deliberately choose handles to obscure information about gender, pretending to be the opposite sex. (For the purposes of this book, I have *invented* handles for the characters I discuss, and I have attempted to connect these handles with their personality style.)

Still, even in this virtually anonymous situation, some subtle clues about the personality of the person writing are available. But becoming aware of them requires paying close attention, perhaps even more attention than in a face-to-face meeting. Even in daily interactions, much of the information we receive about personality characteristics is subliminal. Both in person and on the Internet, our own psychological structure sometimes resists "paying attention" to personality information that is especially significant, information that carries clear evidence of problems to come.

Before they could avoid painful relationships, Jane, Fred and Sarah all had to make an effort to understand their habitual attraction to people who present problems for them. Then they had to learn to pay attention to personality clues in the people they met. Making such observations and connections based on e-mail alone can be very difficult.

THEIR PERSONALITY ATTRACTS YOU

From: Laughter
To: MountainMan

What I like about meeting someone on the Net is that you don't know what he looks like, and he doesn't know what you look like. The relationship is all about what is

happening inside the soul and the mind, and the body doesn't get in the way. I hate the way people make judgments about you based on how you look. I've met people and even fallen in love with someone who I would never have looked at twice at a party.

From: MountainMan
To: Laughter

Oh, that may be fine for some people. But I don't want to end up in the situation of meeting some woman I met online and she turns out to be a real porker. What a person looks like matters to me. I can't help it, I'm just not turned on by fat. And I have met a few women who were very dishonest about how they looked—now I always get a picture first.

From: Laughter
To: MountainMan

I believe that people can fall in love through e-mail because they meet their souls first. People have a tendency to pour out their feelings, their thoughts, their dreams, their fears—through the written word—because that's ALL they have available to convey who they are. If you think that what people look like is the most impor-

**tant consideration, you are missing out on the most
important things in any relationship.**

Many personality traits are evident even through the medium of e-mail. In a general group discussion, one person may repeatedly contradict what others are saying, while another person may be continually responding with anger or taking offense. MountainMan may post many messages about his dislike of overweight women, or his posts may frequently refer to what someone else looks like or what he looks like. In such a case, we can get a general idea of what he might be like in a face-to-face meeting.

The peacemakers among us also make themselves evident in computer discussion forums, as they try to calm the angry ones down or explain a point that was misinterpreted by someone who was offended. Some people regularly intensify debate, while others regularly defuse and minimize disagreements.

Depression and unhappiness are evident in some posts, and in group discussions some individuals repeatedly react with paranoid rage. A small number of participants seem to be actively out of touch with reality. If you are a participant in an ongoing discussion, become familiar with the handles of the other participants. If you pay attention to what they write and how they respond to the others, you can learn a lot about their personalities.

Phaedra wrote to StrongGuy after a couple of exchanges:

From: Phaedra
To: StrongGuy

I just LOVE talking to you. You are so funny, and you always seem to know exactly what I am thinking. It is as though your words were happening inside my HEART, and they ring so true, they make me feel like you and I are SOULMATES. I've always had such trouble really talking to men—I don't think they really understand what I am talking about. But you somehow manage to connect with me on a truly deeper level. Everything you write about seems as though you know me through and through. You are just a WONDERFUL man!

I think about you sometimes as I am falling asleep—I feel so warmed by your caring that I hope for sweet dreams.

After just a few exchanges, this communication is excessively emotional, full of emphatic words, strongly suggesting that Phaedra has romantic fantasies about StrongGuy. If StrongGuy is paying attention, he might notice clues about Phaedra's personality that could predict some of her future behavior. He might realize that she is imagining much more closeness than he is experiencing, that she is romanticizing the relationship as something magical, which has very little to do with StrongGuy's own reality.

On the other hand, if StrongGuy isn't paying attention, he may unconsciously respond to these clues by welcoming the importance Phaedra attaches to him (a gratifying feeling) or by becoming very anxious about it. Depending on his unconscious response to her personality style, he may decide either to communicate with Phaedra further or to avoid her. If he has a tendency to get involved with very emotionally expressive women, he will likely be very attracted to her. If he has previously had failed relationships with very emotionally expressive women, he may well have another relationship failure ahead of him with Phaedra.

From: StrongGuy
To: Phaedra

Ah, Phaedra! I am so glad to hear from you. I thought something was wrong when you didn't reply to my last post for three whole days. I was worried I had said something that offended you, but then you write me and all that time seems like nothing. Your notes make me feel warm all over—I've always had a hard time talking to women, just like you've had a hard time talking to men. Seems like I'm always putting my foot in my mouth, and they go stomping out the door.

I hope I am in your dreams and that you will recognize me there, thinking of you and maybe even dreaming about you myself.

StrongGuy longs for closeness, so he responds to Phaedra's post with increased warmth instead of caution. By doing so, he increases the connectedness between the two of them. He also shows that he gets nervous about relationships and that he cannot tell how his messages are received until she replies. Another hallmark of e-mail communication is the lack of facial feedback and body language that allow you to judge how someone is reacting to what you say. While a delay of three days is brief in terms of written correspondence, in e-mail even such a short delay can be deeply uncomfortable, especially when the writers have been regularly corresponding three or four times a day.

On receiving an e-mail, the relief from such heightened anxiety can be tremendous. The intensity of that relief can easily intensify the importance of the relationship. By regular mail, an actual letter may take days to arrive, and for those who write to pen pals in distant countries, to soldiers in the military or to convicts in prison, the turnaround time can be weeks. Writers of these letters may wait anxiously by the mailbox, and each time the mail comes, they may experience dread, delight or sadness—but that experience happens only once a day. With e-mail, new messages may be sent and received many times a day. The two people involved may be constantly thinking of each other, and message sending may become more important than any other activity.

As in daily life, an e-mail writer may be attracted to someone for "all the wrong reasons." For example, Angel-4 received this e-mail from HillClimber in a book discussion forum:

From: HillClimber
To: Angel-4

I don't know why you always disagree with what I say. Seems to me that you are always trying to promote your own point of view and not paying attention to mine. It is so frustrating to talk to you about literature when you are not as educated and/or as well read as I am but somehow you feel like you can just run right over everything I say.

We might expect Angel-4 to be insulted by this communication and respond to it with anger, to ignore it or to refuse to write to HillClimber ever again. But instead of being insulted, she responds this way:

From: Angel-4
To: HillClimber

I'm so sorry that I keep contradicting you. I know that I haven't got the education you do, and your opinions are tremendously important. I wasn't even trying to contradict you, and I will be much more careful in the future not to do that. I learn so much from the people on this forum and I know I can learn so much from you . . . please don't be mad at me.

From: HillClimber

To: Angel-4

**Okay, kid, don't take it so hard. I know you want to par-
ticipate, and you can certainly learn a lot from these discussions. I'm not mad. Your desire to improve yourself is
admirable, and I have a list of books that I think any
well-educated person ought to read. If you wish, I can
forward the list to you and we can discuss them privately. Tell me more about yourself.**

Both parties to this interaction have told us a great deal
about their personality styles. HillClimber has shown that he
believes himself to be "better than" Angel-4. He is unwilling
to deal with negative feedback from her and possibly from
others on the forum, and he becomes pretty angry when
someone disagrees with him. He has few inhibitions about
attacking Angel-4 personally when he thinks she has inappro-
priately disagreed with him. Angel-4, for her part, shows herself to have low self-esteem concerning her education and her
own opinions. She is apparently quite worried about people
getting angry at her, so she will apologize and take the blame
for events that have led to angry interactions, perhaps even
those for which she was not to blame. She may be a peace-
maker, but she may also be unduly timid, or excessively fearful of anger.

No clues are given here about what either party does for
a living, or what their actual educational level is. Neither
Angel-4 nor HillClimber has demonstrated age, social class or

personal philosophy—and we cannot tell if they smoke or drink heavily, or if they are thin, fat, beautiful or ugly. HillClimber could be either male or female, though in this example I have identified him as male. But within their correspondence they show personality traits that may draw them closer together.

HillClimber has offered to form a private relationship with Angel-4 outside the book discussion forum. Such private communication may create a sense of personal closeness between them. He increases the personal quality by asking more about Angel-4, and if her reply contains enough information that is *unconsciously* appealing to him, they may go on to send one another long messages, not only about books but also about their lives, thoughts, feelings and hopes.

If HillClimber feels that people in his daily life do not adequately value his opinions, he may feel drawn to Angel-4, who has demonstrated to him her willingness to take the blame for negative interactions and who expresses respect for his learning and his opinion. Angel-4 may feel that "if only" she can form a positive relationship with such an "educated and intelligent" man, she will overcome her own perceived lack of these things. If she can bring this man to be kind to her, or to like her, her self-esteem may be at least temporarily improved.

It may be difficult to imagine someone being attracted to a person who is arrogant or who puts them down. In this version of the Cinderella complex, a man or woman who feels inferior or unlovable seeks out a "prince" to pull them up from the ashes and prove to themselves and others that they are indeed worthy. This kind of relationship is not uncommon, but it doesn't produce the result that the Cinderella wishes. Instead of proving that she is lovable, she finds herself put down and once again made to feel inferior or unlovable. No amount of "proof" of her lovability is enough to overcome her deep emotional need for outside approval.

BREAKING DOWN THE BARRIERS TO INTIMACY

The anonymity of e-mail interactions can allow people to behave in ways that they would not in a face-to-face meeting. In fact, it is this very anonymity that breaks down ordinary barriers to intimacy. But electronic conversations also cause problems for intimacy: They leave more room for misunderstanding than do personal conversations, and e-mail exerts less social pressure to control the expression of many emotions, including anger. This problem has resulted in "flaming," an excessively angry and insulting response to someone's message.[2] Flaming happens out of the blue, and it ranges from the short blast of "You ignorant m*therf**ker" to more extensive derogations of the morals, ethics, educational status and probable sexual preferences of the individual being flamed.

HillClimber, for example, instead of sending Angel-4 his "I don't know why you always disagree" message, might have flamed her in the following way: "You ignorant hick. Although you may have sexual experience with farm animals, your moronic ramblings about literature demonstrate your miserable lack of education or experience with anything more elevated than cow-pies. Please spare us your illiterate spewing of opinions." She would have been devastated.

There is little likelihood that he would have spoken to her that way at a party or a lunch meeting. But on the Internet, some people seem to feel that there are no limits on what they can say to a faceless stranger. Like very intimate personal information, an uncensored expression of anger or disagreement is often simpler to send to a stranger who is anonymous than it is to say outright to a stranger who is standing in the same room. E-mail flaming has little likelihood of reaping serious personal consequences—but the same verbal assault in a face-to-face meeting could result in violence.

Unfortunately, even a response that is intended to be only mildly angry or disparaging can come across on the computer screen as hostile or mean. "What an idiot!" can be said lovingly, humorously, angrily or pensively—in person. The vocal inflection can take the sting out of a negative remark and even turn a criticism into a witticism. But on the screen, only the words are amenable to interpretation, and "What an idiot!" will very likely come across as a blood insult. "Flame wars" have resulted from simple misunderstandings of intent, which in person would have been avoided with body language, vocal inflection and eye contact.

The lack of ordinary social controls that allows people to express more anger in e-mail than in daily life also allows them to send unguarded personal information more easily. On the Internet, people frequently discuss sexual problems and personal foibles and share even closely guarded secrets with total strangers. Many people find it easier to ask direct questions about feelings via e-mail than in person, and to answer such questions as well.

In ordinary social interactions, interpersonal distance is a normal experience. Most people have a sense of what is reasonable to discuss with the people around them: what to share with a close girlfriend, versus what to share around the office or with passing acquaintances. But on the Internet, interpersonal distance is difficult, if not impossible, to experience and judge. If you share personal information with someone, you tend to think of them as a friend and to feel closer to them. The more intimate your discussion, the closer you feel. So it becomes easy to think of a faceless person on the Internet in the same way you think of a close friend or lover: as someone you can trust and tell your troubles to.

Since e-mail communication carries so little ordinary social information, is difficult to interpret in terms of emotional intensity and is frequently uncensored in its intimate or emotional content, it creates an atmosphere of great intimacy. By virtue of its anonymity, e-mail can facilitate a level of emotional intimacy that is both emotionally satisfying and emotionally unsettling.

ONE E-MAIL RELATIONSHIP

The following e-mail correspondence progressed from mutual interest in a public discussion to a strong romantic bond. (Remember, the messages here are composites and are not printed in their entirety. [That would require a book-length manuscript all by itself!].)

Cadet is a man in his forties, working as a nurse in Portland, Oregon. Circe is a woman in her mid-thirties, living in Australia and working as a police officer. They met in a Usenet group about travel, but after a few public exchanges they are now communicating privately.

From: Circe
To: Cadet
Subject: Reply to: It's Me Again
Date: 22 September

Hello Cadet!

Yes, it's me again. I hope you don't mind me writing to you so regularly, but it seems like such a long time since I've been able to communicate with someone who's not involved in law enforcement.

You asked how I ended up in law enforcement? Well, it all began in 1976 when I was 16. I had no intention of going to University and found that being at school was inhibiting my ambitions of being a Rock Star (boy was I an idiot). My parents, a couple of understanding persons, gave me 3 options—either go to school, get a job or get out of the house.

It's been my experience that my previous partners (non-law enforcement persons) don't understand what I've been through—and I, being such a self-involved individual, can't help but feel slighted by their apparent lack of concern and understanding—thus another relationship bites the dust.

With my last few relationships I thought someone in the same line of work would surely be able to understand. As it has turned out, I've been the one doing the understanding—at quite an emotional cost to myself—and they've been the ones doing the self-involved thing.

It's 9 am here at the moment, about 70 degrees, no wind, and a beautiful sunny day. There's the smell of jasmine wafting in through the window, and I've got the day off. I think I might take myself off to the beach and work on some melanomas.

Oh drat! There was the phone ringing and I answered it— they want me to come into work. I can't believe I said I would do it. I should have gone to the beach earlier.

Circe

From: Cadet
To: Circe
Subject: The Search for Signs of Intelligent Life
Date: 22 September

Hello, Circe!

>>Yes, it's me again. I hope you don't mind me writing to you so regularly . . . <<

Far from it; I am enjoying our correspondence immensely.

For myself, I never wanted to be a rock star . . . no, I

wanted to be the next Woody Guthrie or Pete Seeger. I used to play my guitar and sing my original songs in coffeehouses (for a brief spell I was world famous in Juneau, Alaska) and even once at a big festival at summer solstice in Anchorage. You may note that I grew up in Alaska. Those dreams died fairly hard; I shifted over to poetry when it became clear I would not be "discovered" in Anchorage. I had quite the pile of rejection slips . . . ah well, at 19, one is ever optimistic.

>>should have stuck with the Rock Star thing.<<

Well, it can't be too late for that <g>—look at Tina Turner! Still boogying at who can tell how old . . . But I hope you've been practicing the guitar this past 16 years. Or the drums or whatever.

We had a wonderful fall day here . . . sunny and cool, with a hint of dying leaves and woodsmoke in the air. I took apart the garden and got it ready for winter, and then I went out to buy some winter clothes (can't greet a new season without new clothes) and generally tried to fill the day with pleasant things. I've been on call this weekend, carrying the beeper and the cell phone, and I've another weekend ahead of being on call, then I am dropping my beeper down a well. I am getting a 4 day trip to the beach in mid-October; no melanomas for me, just rain and wind and surf and NO PHONES. I plan to take my CD player and pig out on Jethro Tull and the Moody Blues.

>>I answered it—they want me to come into work.<<

**Never answer the phone when you aren't on call . . .
never never never. Trust me, on this one I am an expert.**

**Hope you get to the beach soon yourself—take care and
write whenever you darned well feel like it.**

**Best,
Cadet**

Already, Circe and Cadet are talking about their childhood
dreams and exchanging a good deal of emotional information
about themselves. The easy friendliness between them started
with the public discussions and is becoming more intimate fairly
rapidly. As Circe tells Cadet about her life, she grows more
attached to him and demonstrates in the next few notes that she
is thinking about him and what he is writing to her.

She has begun to talk about her difficulties in previous
relationships, from which he may learn important information about what problems might arise in his relationship with
her. Some characteristics are already evident in even these few
interactions: Circe has some ambivalence about her job as it
intersects with her relationships, and Cadet demonstrates a
poetic bent and perhaps some sadness about his lost dreams.

Over the course of perhaps a week, this interaction progresses from friendly exchanges to a more romantic and fan-
tasy-based relationship.

From: Cadet
To: Circe
Subject: Not to worry
Date: 25 September

Hello, Circe!

Please pardon me if this reply seems slow—my computer attempted suicide and is at the computer hospital being treated. It may be back in a week, maybe not. So I haven't been able to check my messages for a bit.

>> Are you familiar with that Kris Kristofferson song "Me and Bobby McGee," in particular the line "I'd trade all of my tomorrows for just one single yesterday"? Well I can't count the number of sleepless nights I've had wishing that I could do just that.<<

I know the Janis Joplin version of this song . . . and I have been finishing it in my mind: "I'd trade all my tomorrows for just one yesterday—of holding Bobby's body close to mine." But I can't see it, really. Even at this point in my life where I begin to look at getting older and realizing that those young vivid years are nearly behind me, I can't see trading off tomorrow for some lost love. But I can see trading off tomorrow for some lost self.

Trying to make sense of the world, trying to balance optimism and pessimism—I think that is the most important

struggle that most philosophers never even approach dealing with.

>>By then I hope to have my commercial pilot's license and then I will be heading up north to the tropics to fly tourists around the various islands on the Great Barrier Reef.<<

How much time do you have before you get your license? The year 2000 is only a few years away. I have had major fantasies of getting a big catamaran and working off the islands of the Grand Caymans. There is a wonderful place there—they call it Ray's Stingray City, and it is a huge long sandbar that the stingrays hang out at. Everyday catamarans full of tourists (I among them once) come out to feed the rays and marvel at these giant sea creatures that are so graceful in the water. I figured that one would only have to have about 70 tourists per week to pay off the boat and live; after that, it's just hang a line off the side and live off the fish. I love that one.

Another of my fantasies is to get a little house on the Oregon coast, right where you can hear the waves crashing up on the beach, get a big ol' dog and a part-time job (probably at the post office), and the rest of the time walk on the beach and be a writer.

>> I can visualise Portland and how it must be as the summer fades and winter, using autumn as a colourful distraction, quietly slips in.<<

This is always a strange time of year for me. I find myself longing for the new beginnings of going back to school; autumn will likely always mean that to me. It makes me restless, yearning for something hard to pin down. Then October sets in and I settle down again (I hope).

Been a pretty difficult day today, with trying to deal with my computer and this yearning for something unknown. I went out with a friend to dinner and we ended up talking about all the other times in our lives we had felt this need to make some new beginning and what came of that. On the whole, it was a satisfying end to a dismal day.

Take care, Circe,
Cadet

From: Circe
To: Cadet
Subject: Reply to: Ray's Stingray City
Date: 26 September

Hi Cadet,

Your fantasy of buying a catamaran and cruising the islands off the Grand Caymans is so good that I've decided to steal it from you. What has prompted my theft of your fantasy? Well, it was your question relating to how long is my boyfriend going to Italy for. It made me think about something I'm doing my level best to forget. Hence if I can indulge myself in fantasy, I can't think of the unpleasantness I am striving to blot out.

David is going to Italy for a year which, in terms of my life, is only 1/37th of my entire time on the planet. One would think that such a short period of time should not cause me much concern, but there are other issues involved that make twelve months seem like an eternity.

It was only a matter of very little time from when we moved in together that we went from being lovers to being cohabitants. This did not please me, but I seemed powerless to stop David from rebuilding the barriers that he had brought with him to the police department when I first met him.

David started studying Italian, and I started studying for my commercial pilot's license—rather than confront the situation, both of us opted for the "substitute the love that is missing with anything that takes up time" option.

Around April this year David gained a scholarship to study in Florence for one year. I was just getting ready to finally divorce my husband (we had been separated for a few years). It was just a very bad time for all this to be happening. I foolishly, and off-handedly, said to David, "Well if you want to go, just go." David was not without responsibility in this relationship downfall, though. Re my divorce he said, "Look, I'm not the person you should talk to about this. I've got enough problems of my own." Mr. Sensitivity, eh? So I continued with my flying and trying to sort out my divorce whilst David continued with his studying.

I have been in a relationship of some kind since I was 14—long term, short term, a few one-night stands, and frankly, I've not found anything as satisfying as the committed relationships—even when they fail miserably. Semipermanent relationships usually mean that one person has more or less commitment than the other, and as a result someone gets hurt. Therefore, for me, it's either full on or not at all.

So, I hope you can see why Ray's Stingray City is so important to me. The Oregon Coast one isn't bad either, but I do prefer the warmer weather.

Re the "Me and Bobby McGee" song—it wasn't until I read your last letter that I considered that I may be trying to reclaim a lost love, or even a lost version of me. In just the stroke of a pen (or should I say "in just a few key strokes") you have given me a valuable insight into myself at, what I would consider to be, a crucial time in my life. Sure it might not solve all or any of my current problems, but the fact that you have taken the time to share your wisdom with me (basically a total stranger) has meant a great deal to me. I only hope that I will be able to return the favour someday.

Now I know how to sign this off.

With much gratitude and eternally in your debt,
Circe

Increasingly, personal information is being exchanged concerning emotional dissatisfactions, relationship problems and general information about daily activities. Cadet is in some sense using Circe as a sounding board for his feelings, much as he would probably have used a diary or journal in the past. He is talking about his feelings more readily to her than he would to someone in his daily life.

In this interchange Cadet and Circe are also beginning to build a fantasy of "being together." Several of the people who responded to my questionnaire said that as they and their Internet correspondent exchanged fantasies of being together, they began to truly feel attached to each other. Writing about such fantasies made the experiences seem almost real—with the warmth and caring that they *wished* would be there supplied from their own imagination. The transition from simple fantasies of spending time together to fantasies of romantic "dates" seemed to move the relationships to a deeper level. One man said that he took such pleasure in writing these fantasies that he was careful to include a new one every day in his correspondence.

As for Cadet, he is expressing a sense of loneliness and emotional need that Circe is beginning to respond to. She is feeling needed, and that she is able to talk to Cadet about her own loneliness and dissatisfactions. Sharing such feelings can be very difficult in face-to-face interactions. For some people, the very act of writing out their experiences brings these feelings to their conscious attention in a way that would not happen in ordinary conversation.

Both Cadet and Circe are writing their correspondence in the diary mode. As described in chapter 1, writing to another person as though in a diary enhances the sense of intimacy. Without being able to see each other in person, they are still able to feel connected and even romantic toward each other. The facelessness of the other person—the "diary"—allows the fantasy of closeness to strengthen.

Circe is having fantasies about what Cadet is like as a person. She praises his "wisdom" and sees him as having a special access to understanding her, which allows her to tell him about her painful experiences. Cadet, in turn, feels special in Circe's eyes—a feeling that is gratifying to them both. Not everyone can appreciate one's wisdom—and finding someone who does can be elevating to the spirit.

If Cadet is inclined toward taking care of people, then Circe's relationship problems may appeal to him, since she seems to be in pain and in need of being taken care of. If Circe is seeking escape from her daily life, Cadet's fantasies can help provide that escape.

From: Circe
To: Cadet
Subject: Reply to: Not to Worry
Date: 27 September

Hi Cadet,

I must admit that I am becoming a bit curious as to the identity of the person to whom I am corresponding on such a regular basis. At the moment all I know is that you probably speak with an American accent. From your talk about Pete Seeger, I imagine you to look something like him—only younger and alive, of course <g>. [<g> means "grin."]

>>This is always a strange time of year for me . . . It makes me restless, yearning for something hard to pin down. Then October sets in and I settle down again (I hope).<<

Please don't think me presumptuous, but have you ever considered not settling down again—perhaps there is a genuine and real reason for this "hard to pin down" thing that you are yearning/searching for. On the other hand maybe it's just a seasonal thing—you know, the body changing its chemistry to adapt to the climatic changes makes you feel like something is not quite right. In any event I am the last person to give advice. Any inspection of my rather unsuccessful attempts to live a normal life would indicate that I probably don't have a clue as to what I'm doing or saying.

"Been a pretty difficult day today,"
"it's been a long and somewhat difficult day"
"On the whole, it was a satisfying end to a dismal day."

The three above mentioned quotes were written by yourself during the early hours of the morning—as you can see they contain two difficults, one dismal and a yearning for something unknown. As it is fast approaching early morning here I can certainly relate to the same feelings. It saddens me to hear that you too have such days—from what I know about you, albeit only a sketchy outline of yourself, I feel that you have all the things that I desire. You have a nice place to live, a challenging career, and you seem to be at peace with your life choices. I have none of those things.

I have been riding an emotional rollercoaster for the past twenty years and still haven't worked out how to get off it. From what I can glean from your previous letters, you have obviously experienced the emotional rollercoaster—perhaps you have just forgotten what it is like. From one who is still on it, I can assure you that it's still the same old rollercoaster. If you were to get back on it, I'm sure you would find that the only thing that has changed is you. Having said that, the rollercoaster is the same as the catamaran—there's always room for one more. Obviously the decision to ride or not to ride is yours to make.

Anyway, I hope I have been placing the correct interpretation on your letters and that I haven't offended you to the point where I will not hear from you again. All I can say in my defense is that I have been awake since 4:45 a.m. yesterday morning, and fatigue has a tendency to make me write the first things that come to mind.

I hope by the time you read this that you have had an exceptionally GREAT day, that your computer comes back to you in one piece, and that you save a few lives.

Must go and try to sleep—won't be easy as I'm still hyped up.

P.S. I'm not really this flaky, I'm just tired.

Fondest regards
Circe

Circe is seeking more reality-based images of Cadet, while revealing that she herself is constructing some fantasy images as well. Their interactions are becoming more personal, more complex and more intimate. Even as she is expressing her own unhappiness, Circe is also very responsive to clues that Cadet is having some painful emotional experiences too. Her responsiveness to that pain and to his internal world are deepening the relationship, enhancing their closeness.

Circe's willingness to talk directly to Cadet about her perceptions of him may be due to the sense of safety and distance that e-mail imparts. She confronts him about what may be going on with him in a way that most people reserve for their closest friends. She, in fact, is feeling closer to him as the days go by. Still, these letters are essentially friendly and supportive; although the sense of intimacy is increased, really romantic feelings are not evident. Circe signs her note "fondest regards," another signal that she is feeling more personally involved with Cadet.

From: Cadet
To: Circe
Subject: Reply to: Working too hard
Date: 28 September

Circe:

There is a wonderful cartoon strip in the daily papers here called "Rose," and over time we have come to know that Rose has this biker chick persona that sometimes sweeps over her (as she has a child persona) and there are situa-

tions or activities that bring that out (so that she is drawn in one panel as her usual self and the next as a biker chick). One day she is walking with her mother, and they both turn into biker chicks in response to something (I forget what). I laughed out loud at the breakfast table—it was as though she was saying "every woman has a biker chick inside her." That character dresses in black leather, is young and unencumbered, attractive and slightly dangerous. She reminded me of your studying to get a pilot's license—maybe you're the one with the biker inside you and I'm just struggling with plain old midlife crisis.

So let me tell you my motorcycle fantasy—you can play, too. We are riding along the Alaska-Canada Highway in midsummer. Although it is nearly midnight, the sun is low, but the daylight is still with us, edging the huge range of mountains before us with gold. The road is empty but for us, and stretches out before us like a gray ribbon looping over the foothills. The fireweed is in bloom, filling the meadows with tall pink flowers and the air with their sweet fragrance. You are holding me tight around the waist, and I feel your heartbeat at my back. At just that moment that we crest the hill, riding with the wind rushing around us, the moon rises full over the mountains.

Some nights when I cannot sleep, the daydream of riding along the highway soothes me to sleep. I hope you are not working this weekend. Tell me about the beach you like to go to.

Fondly,
Cadet

From: Circe
To: Cadet
Subject: Reply to: Working too hard
Date: 30 September

Hi Cadet,

May I start with the segment of your last letter that most appealed? "So let me tell you my motorcycle fantasy"—I can just picture it. Only problem is that I was riding along and just starting to soak up the moon rays when "pouf" there goes the motorcycle, right out from under me, and I'm sitting back in front of the computer. Quite the lonely letdown.

>> But even if you can't imagine it, I rode a motorcycle in my teens<< Actually, I can imagine it. It really goes along with the fantasy I have about you: you in leathers, with long hair and a really well-sculpted body . . . oops . . . didn't mean to bring up THAT fantasy <g>.

I will describe the beach I like to go to when next I write. It takes a lot of describing.

Holding you tight,
Circe

From: Cadet
To: Circe
Subject: Moonlight and Motorcycles
Date: 30 September

Circe:

Well, let me momentarily continue the motorcycle journey, Circe. As the brief Alaskan night falls, we approach a lake. The water is completely still, and we get off our bike to stand on the shore. Like Hansel and Gretel in the woods, we hold hands so we won't lose each other. The moon makes a silver path along the water, and we can see the rings spreading out from where the fish are nibbling skeeters. Loons are calling out their eerie birdsong from the banks and at our feet is an island of water lilies, green and gold in daylight, but silver and gray in the edge of the moon's path. The air is cooling slowly, and the smell of unfolding birch leaves fills the air. Turning away from the light, at just that moment, a huge snow white owl floats towards us in absolute silence. We hold our breath in awe.

I see I have several more notes from you—I haven't checked my e-mail since last night. More when I read the rest.

Fondly,
Cadet

The motorcycle fantasy begins a powerful fantasy relationship between these two people. Several couples have told me that they wrote about fantasies of spending time together as a way of communicating their increasingly warm feelings about each other. The fantasies tended to be about "a perfect moment, a romantic or beautiful moment where you would say to yourself that it was good to be alive for that moment." They are also a way of trying on the romantic possibilities of a relationship, to see if the other person responds appropriately. Would they like the activity, the moment, and would they like the writer and the writing of it?

With the phrase "a really well-sculpted body," Circe has "upped the ante" by bringing in a more directly sexual fantasy about Cadet. Although he does not respond directly to this part of the note, it sets the stage for an increasingly romantic and potentially sexual relationship.

Because of the geographic distance that lies between them, actual sex is not possible. Some couples go on from their romantic fantasies into fantasy sex, exchanging erotic or even frankly graphic portrayals of the sexual acts they imagine. Obviously, the transition from the friendly to the romantic to the sexual is a delicate one to navigate, and even in relationships where the two partners have become romantic and feel themselves to be in love, frankly sexual content may remain "off-limits."

From: Cadet
To: Circe
Subject: Reply to: Someone up there must like me!
Date: 04 October

Hello, Circe!

Sitting by the lake in the short Alaskan darkness, we see a rowboat on the shore. Very quietly, because the night is so very quiet a hundred miles from all other humans, we pull the boat out into the water and row to the center of the lake. We lean up against each other for warmth, I have my arm around you to hold you close. The sense of waiting becomes almost intolerable, until finally the sun begins to rise, and little wisps of fog on the surface catch the light and seem to have a light of their own.

The sky begins to lighten, first white, then gold, and finally opens up into a brilliant blue while the lake is still in the mountain shadow. The smell of the new morning is breathtaking; as fresh as the newest morning in the first day of the world. When we lean over the side of the boat to look at the water, still as glass, we see the reflection of our two faces, and above them reflects the full moon, still in the sky, sharing with the sun. We reach out to touch the reflections and our hands meet in the sparkling water. Breathless from the transformation of night to day, I turn to you and our lips meet. . . .

Dreaming while awake, Cadet

Cadet and Circe made a tacit agreement to explore fantasies of being together, and the fantasies have moved toward romantic physical closeness. They are ready to communicate outside the computer. In the next chapters, we will look at relationships that move on to romance and love.

CHAPTER 3

In Love Before You Know It

LOVE AT FIRST BYTE FOR TEXAS COP ON INTERNET

LONDON—A Texas policewoman who fell in love with a British store manager while surfing the Internet has flown to Britain to marry her high-tech Romeo. It was love at first byte for Fort Worth patrolwoman Donna Qalawi when she spent hours on the global information superhighway talking to computer-mad Craig Bottomley. Qalawi, leaving Texas for the first time, has now given up her job to fly to Britain and marry Craig without ever having seen him before. "I know it sounds crazy but I knew from just talking to him on the computer that I loved him—and after meeting him I know I made the right decision," Qalawi told reporters Sunday.

"My family all think it is wonderful, so I have given up my job to be with him. I know we will make a great couple." Print shop manager Bottomley only broke the news to his father 30 minutes before his fiancée's plane landed. "He was a bit shocked when I told him."

REUTERS

INNOCENT BEGINNINGS

It's four A.M., and John D.'s computer is still brightly lit. While his wife sleeps soundly, he communicates enthusiastically in the chat room to his friends. Especially, he talks to his new friend with the handle Starchild. In the last three weeks alone, after work and late into the night, he has spent about forty hours talking to Starchild.

During his first foray into the chat rooms, John entertained himself by reading the public messages back and forth between the other participants. He didn't participate much, but occasionally he would respond to a comment, and soon he got more familiar with the other "characters." They were only characters to him because they had handles instead of real names, like Pooh or FunnyGuy or Hardcore. He chose his own handle, Warrior, then had to add a number to it because so many other people on the board had the same handle.

As Warrior8, John recognized more characters, and so when Starchild wrote him a private note with a funny and somewhat sexual comment, he responded readily. Over the course of several days, he wrote privately to Starchild to the exclusion of all his other usual activities. They began to send e-mail back and forth, and even while he was working, he would check his e-mail many times each day, with increasing eagerness to hear from Starchild.

From: Warrior8
To: Starchild

I have been having a hard day today. There are so many things to do and my supervisor is kind of a dolt. He has been on my case about this project, and he doesn't even know what the project is about. Like that guy in the Dilbert cartoons, we could probably tell him an Etch-A-Sketch was a computer screen and he wouldn't even notice.

It sounds like you had a hard day yesterday, too. I feel sad when I hear that you are so unhappy at your job—I wish I could be there to comfort you. We could take a walk along the river and escape all this together. I would buy you a balloon just to see you laugh, and we would sit at a sidewalk cafe and drink espresso in the sun.

Sometimes when I think about my life, I have dreams of just leaving everything behind and going to New York. I've never told anyone this before, but I always wanted to be a composer, and I could just play the piano and not have to deal with the daily responsibilities of my life.

You sound so lonely, sometimes. Haven't you got a boyfriend or someone to spend time with?

Warrior8

From: Starchild
To: Warrior8

Dearest Warrior8! You could live in New York and write music, and I would work at the cafe nearby. In the evenings, we would walk along Fifth Avenue and buy our dinner at some little deli—we would be poor but living life to its fullest. A wonderful daydream.

No, I don't have a boyfriend. I just split up with my boyfriend of six years, and it's very hard. I sit home some evenings and just cry—I spend this time on the computer to avoid spending time just weeping; your notes are a real comfort to me. It just amazes me still that he left—we were talking about getting married and then suddenly, he has to have "space." I hate it when they tell me they need "space." It's just a code word for wanting to get away from me. All men don't fear commitment, do they? It's like that old joke about how you get rid of cockroaches in your apartment—you ask them to make a commitment.

I feel so lonely without him. We were having a lot of fights toward the end, and I couldn't seem to leave it alone. I couldn't stop myself from asking him about getting married even when we were having some awful time. I guess, now that I think about it, that I was really starting to feel him slipping away and I wanted to somehow tie him to me. Nothing like impending departure to

> **bring those thoughts of marriage to the fore, eh, Warrior?**
>
> **Love,**
> **Starchild**

These notes back and forth were very different—pleasantly so—from John's everyday interactions. In response to Starchild's questions, he revealed painful events from his childhood that had troubled him for years. He had never told anyone about them, not even his wife, and yet it was so easy with Starchild. He wrote her twenty times a day.

> **From: Warrior8**
> **To: Starchild**
>
> **My relationship with my wife is sometimes like that. I want to have children, but she has two from her first marriage and doesn't want any more. I keep dreaming of somehow being a better father to my kids than my dad was to me. He left when I was three, and I have never known what it would be like to grow up with a dad—with your OWN dad, I mean. I love my step-kids, but they aren't really mine, just like my step-dad wasn't really my own dad. I always felt that he would go away just like my real dad did—**
>
> **I don't know about that commitment problem . . . after all, wouldn't you succeed in driving away only the MALE**

cockroaches? <g> But there is something really upsetting about the feeling of getting more distant while the other person is trying to get closer. It seems to make everything worse, just like you describe in your relationship with your boyfriend.

I have been wanting to ask you this for a while now—would you mind telling me what you look like? It is hard to just write to a faceless someone, and I have to say I have made up a picture in my mind of what you look like.

Love,
Warrior8

As the feelings of intimacy and closeness grew, John's wife, Paula, was unaware that anything was happening. She had no idea that John was writing to another woman. When he was at his computer, she imagined that he was working or "checking his e-mail" or playing computer games. But he was spending more and more time doing it, and recently he had been coming to bed very late. This began to worry her.

John reassured himself that what he was doing was no big deal. He was just writing to someone on the Internet—he didn't even know her real name, had never actually seen her, and so he couldn't imagine that there was a problem. Even when the notes between Starchild and himself became increasingly sexual and emotionally intimate, he still thought there was no problem. But he soon found that the time he spent with his wife was boring compared with the time he spent writing to Starchild. Even when he was with his family, he thought about Starchild. He couldn't wait to check his e-mail in the evenings.

At one point Starchild went on vacation without her computer, and John grew depressed. As days went by without her e-mail, he felt himself dragging around the office and gloomy at home. He couldn't get interested in anything else, and his days without Starchild's "company" seemed gray and empty. He realized with a shock that his contact with her had become the entire focus of his days, and that nothing else was as interesting or important to him.

When he returned, he gave Starchild his phone number—he just wanted to hear her voice. In addition to e-mail, they began to talk on the phone. Sometimes their phone conversations lasted for hours, either late at night while his wife was sleeping or during the day while she was gone. John paid the phone bill himself to avoid any questions about the long-distance charges. Starchild asked John to send her a photograph, and she sent him her picture.

Starchild lived in North Carolina and John lived in Los Angeles, but he began to think of ways they might meet. Their conversations were increasingly filled with fantasies and plans about getting together. One day he realized that he was as deeply in love with Starchild as he had ever been with anyone—even without meeting her. In his mind, their relationship was even deeper, more intense and intimate, and more emotionally satisfying than the one he had with his wife.

NO EARLY WARNING SYSTEM

In everyday life, most married people interact with men and women who are attractive and talented and interesting, but they find ways to manage their emotions to avoid extramarital involvement. Ordinary defense mechanisms help—like avoiding spending a lot of time with an attractive person. At work, John would have avoided having lunch regularly with an attractive woman in his office because he would have known that it could create problems. The strangest aspect of his online relationship with Starchild was the fact that he had no idea it was going anywhere important. The ordinary clues that would have told him he and Starchild were becoming too intimate were not present—until the attachment was *already* strong.

In face-to-face contact the level of closeness that is required before a couple exchanges really personal information varies. Some people are comfortable talking openly about deeply felt emotions almost immediately, but most people need a period of time to grow closer before they feel comfortable enough to reveal intimate information. The process of revealing that information in itself may enhance the intimacy—or it can be a warning if one of the parties is not comfortable with that degree of closeness.

When it comes to online communication, our culture is still clueless. We have not yet established patterns of behavior to manage the emotional impact of communicating with faceless individuals. Online communication facilitates a great deal of projection of fantasies and feelings onto unknown and unseen persons. The anonymity creates a kind of "masked ball" effect—a feeling that things may be said free of ordinary restrictions on behavior and speech. It allows some people to try out new facets of themselves on strangers, and others, like John and Starchild, to express previously hidden yearnings.

In the most ordinary sense, we haven't even learned how to tell when someone's notes get "too personal" too soon, because we're used to relying so heavily on physical information to tell that. In person, when someone of the opposite sex sits too close, makes too intense eye contact or asks really searching intimate questions, we know what that means, and we can therefore choose to draw back. If an attractive co-worker brushed against John as she walked past him, he would think of Paula and move away, feeling that "it made my skin crawl." If a man Starchild didn't know well put his arm around her shoulders, she might feel physically threatened or intruded upon.

But as John sat alone at night before his computer, no such physical information—no "skin crawling"—alerted him that things were heating up between Starchild and him. It was easy for him to reassure himself that their relationship was not meaningful because she lived so far away. He would say to himself, "We'll never meet, so there's no chance of any problems arising from this. It's just writing letters." He would have had a much harder time persuading himself that it was acceptable to have lunch every day with an attractive woman, to meet her after work and to go out with her without his wife's knowledge. The woman's physical presence would have made it clear that he was acting in a way that was dangerous to his marriage, and that he needed to make a choice about what he wanted.

But before John understood what was happening with Starchild, he was already deeply attached to her. Almost against his will, he arranged to meet her at a restaurant in her hometown in North Carolina.

FACE-TO-FACE MEETINGS

Anxiety is a hallmark of face-to-face meetings between lovers who have only known each other on the Internet. Moving from the screen to a café changes all the rules of the relationship and

reveals deceptions and misrepresentations that have been easy
to hide. As John prepared to meet Starchild, he was overwhelmed with fear; he wondered if she would really be the person he imagined, or if he would live up to the images she had
constructed of him.

Fear of being inadequate, of being rejected, of being completely unsuited to each other—these anxieties are not an
issue as long as the relationship stays on the screen. As noted
earlier, the meeting is not a truly "blind date" that you can
shrug off if things don't go well. If you have flown to another city to meet someone that you've spent months talking to
over the Internet, you have a distinct investment in the outcome of the date.

In many cases these anxieties are lessened when the meeting finally happens. Unless one person finds something
extremely objectionable in the other or there was deliberate
misrepresentation, the meeting will likely be mutually plea-
surable, since the steady stream of online messages has pre-
programmed them to like each other. The intensity of the intimacy, and the frequency and pervasiveness of communication, are very compelling, so much so that in some cases the
first meeting leads to sex.

In most cases, however, couples converse animatedly and
further confirm their relationship. They may—or may not—
share information with each other that could torpedo the relationship. They may not mention a spouse or significant other
who is waiting back home. As in other relationships in daily
life, they may not mention a drug addiction, gambling problems or financial difficulties.

Some people succumb to the temptation to describe themselves in highly idealized ways. HillClimber described himself
to Angel-4 as "extremely attractive," but when they finally

met, she found him to be "a kind of a gargoyle-looking man—
he was very tall, and I guess he was well built, but man! His
face was really weirdly misshapen. Hadn't he ever looked in a
mirror?"

For his part, HillClimber was also very disappointed by
his meeting with Angel-4. Although she had described herself
as overweight, in his perception she was morbidly obese.
Although he had expected her to be less educated than he and
to have a lower social status, he was appalled by her style of
dress and appearance, which placed her—in his eyes—several
rungs down the social ladder. While another man might have
found Angel-4 appealing and another woman might have
found HillClimber attractive, the two of them were completely unable to have erotic feelings for each other.

These examples may seem extreme—some might argue
that people really aren't *that* unable to deal with social differences, and that the meeting of souls is more important than
the physical appearance. But erotic connection is not rational.
Without sexual attraction to the other person, romance comes
to a crashing halt.

Based on sexual chemistry, a personal meeting can either
destroy or strengthen a computer relationship. The physical
meeting between HillClimber and Angel-4 shut down their
relationship as though a door had slammed. But when Cadet
and Circe exchanged photographs, they simply modified their
ongoing fantasies accordingly. The exchange of photographs
caused no glaring problems, since their emotional relationship
was already strong enough that they could make allowances
and find attractive traits in each other's appearance. When
such couples meet, their attachment is enhanced and they connect easily.

UNITED BY A COMMON CAUSE

Wendy and Karl first started talking to each other on the Internet about saving whales. Karl, a twenty-six-year-old man living in Denmark, spent much of his time reading the English-language Usenet groups. In one environmental forum he read several of Wendy's thoughtful messages and felt that "here was a woman who got right to the heart of the matter." She understood the problem well and cared passionately about it. He'd already known people who cared, and even some ardent advocates of this important cause, but Wendy, in his opinion, exemplified the best of both.

So he sent her an admiring message, posting it publicly, where anyone could read it. She responded privately. They continued to correspond privately while still posting messages on the Usenet group. "She told me about her life and her commitment to the whales," Karl told me. "She was a real activist and a bright, funny person too!" Karl and Wendy began writing to each other every day. The fact that twenty-four-year-old Wendy lived in California only added to their mutual interest.

"I usually picked up her messages in the morning, and when I didn't get mail from her, I really felt let down," said Karl. "I worried about her and wondered if she was safe. I'd log on every hour to see if she was just sending me mail late that day." If he received no mail at all, he got depressed and cranky and didn't feel like doing much. He worried that she'd never write to him again. He wondered (as he frequently did in relationships) if he had done something wrong. He thought about her constantly, wondering what she looked like, what her apartment was like, and what she would think of him if they ever met.

What Karl didn't know was that Wendy was wondering the same things. She was very drawn to Karl's intuitive understanding of the same issues with which she was concerned. She loved his witty sayings that were also full of depth and meaning. Although they lived on different continents, she was beginning to feel deeply attached to him. Sometimes she reproached herself: How could she be attracted to this guy on the Internet, someone she'd never met and who lived in another country? What if he was some kind of weird geek or a sex fiend or criminal?

Even as she worried, however, she believed that she truly "knew" Karl, that she had made contact with his truest, innermost self and that he was not a weirdo or a criminal. To another online friend, Wendy wrote, "You can perceive, through this imperfect medium, enough to tell a friend or a lover when you see one!" Her friend wrote, "Well, I think if you've been honest about yourself with your online friend, then you can pretty well gauge the reaction to meeting you. I don't think people can 'hide' the real self for very long at all. I know a lot of people online better than I've known almost *anybody* offline. I know more about their inner lives and their thoughts and dreams and fears."

The presumption of honesty is significant on the Internet. Even though some people on the Internet do not tell the truth about themselves, two people who are writing back and forth usually assume that the other is being honest. (In chapter 8 we will look at the issue of deceptive relationships.)

Wendy couldn't resist Karl's caring and insightful messages and didn't want to let him go, so she kept writing to him. And he kept responding to her. "He was so unlike anyone else I'd ever met," she told me. "I almost felt like I could know his soul from the beautiful words he put down and that ran across my monitor screen." She found herself saving his messages and rereading them later. She printed out the especially nice ones. She "projected" fantasies onto Karl, imagining that he really was the person she daydreamed about when she read his notes. Her daydream of a kind, caring man of wit and intelligence may have been close to the truth, but without face-to-face contact, her daydream must still be defined as a "fantasy."

Karl asked her what she looked like and told her that he knew she must be beautiful because of her words. Wendy didn't feel that she was beautiful—maybe average. But even when she stalled and delayed, he kept pressing her for a photo. What should she do? She was filled with agonies of indecision. Don't expect a waiflike thin person, she warned him. Finally one day she decided, "Okay, if he hates me, he hates me!" and she sent a scanned photo of herself to Karl, letting out a deep breath after the computer told her the file was sent.

About a day later, Karl sent Wendy a photo of himself. She opened the file excitedly, eager to finally see what he looked like. He had a nice smile, she saw, but his hair seemed to be thinning a lot, even though he was only twenty-six. Wendy usually didn't like it when men combed their hair over the top, as if they could hide their baldness. And she couldn't tell what color his eyes were! She'd have to ask him. He didn't look like the men she was usually attracted to—he was kind of a string bean. But what a sweet man he was! Wendy was still hooked on him.

Karl had been thrilled to finally receive Wendy's photo, after all that resistance. Okay, she was a little on the chunky side, and he usually liked women who were slender. But she looked at the camera directly, just as she seemed to meet life directly. Karl was hooked too. The photos had not significantly changed their feelings about each other. Karl and Wendy would not have been attracted to each other had they met some other way, but the warmth and closeness of their computer relationship made it possible for them to overlook or override their usual physical attraction patterns.

THE PROGRESSION OF EMOTIONS

Although people differ in their feelings and reactions when they "fall in love online," many couples feel important and cherished and valued by their online partner. They are excited that this other person cares about the same issues or has the same sense of humor. Like teenagers who want friends who share their interest in a particular rock 'n' roll band, adults seek people who share their own interests and beliefs. The fact that Wendy now cared about what was going on in Karl's daily life and the things that bothered him created a special intimacy.

After reading a message, the receiver may begin to compose in her mind what she'd like to say to him, and to *anticipate* what he is likely to say to her. She may carry on a running conversation with him in her mind. In a way, she carries his image around in her head. The image is subject to whatever her fantasies make of it—and at his end, he does the same thing.

The actual writing of the messages helps increase this sense of attachment. A great deal of pleasure can be had from feeling that you have put your best foot forward. Writing letters on a computer, with its opportunities to think about and edit what you are writing, allows a person to appear as interesting, as knowledgeable and as witty as they are able to be.

One man involved in an online romance told me, "I felt so clever, just so funny—the sending was as much of a high as the receiving. It became the thing I thought about all day long, as I waited for a reply, as I thought about my replies. My first thought on awakening was of her."

When Wendy noticed news items and articles in popular magazines that Karl might be interested in, she clipped them for him. She read books she thought he would like and told him about them. When she saw a television show she thought he would enjoy, she told him about it in case he had the opportunity to see it in Denmark someday. In other words, Karl was constantly in her thoughts. Their e-mail messages ran for pages, incorporating several ongoing conversations. Because of the time difference, their message exchanges were less frequent than those of some other online couples, but both spent their days thinking about their messages and each other.

This process is not unlike the process of falling in love in ordinary life, or what's referred to on the Internet as "3-D." In person as well as on the Internet, most couples find that as their relationship progresses, they think about each other constantly, pay attention to things that the other might be interested in and to places and events that are connected to the relationship. On the other hand, most 3-D couples are not able to call each other on the phone twenty times a day, and if they did, the relationship would likely begin to go downhill!

IDEAL COMMUNICATION?

Calling on the phone is actually an intrusive act—the call demands the person's immediate attention, takes them away from a business meeting, pulls them out of the shower, interrupts their favorite TV show. Even leaving a message on an answering machine can be intrusive and frustrating—it may be too late to call back, or the other person may now be unavailable. If one person in a couple were to call twenty times in a day, the other person might feel that something weird was going on—that their partner was obsessed, excessively needy or just plain thoughtless.

But in e-mail communication, these issues are not significant. There is no problem with intrusion or call-backs—each person checks their e-mail when they choose, and replies when it is convenient. Rather than intruding, e-mail gives them a powerful sense of being in control. One telephone call encompasses an entire conversation, but an e-mail conversation requires multiple messages. By e-mail, twenty messages in a day is not remarkable, weird or needy—it simply represents the give-and-take of an ideal conversation, a conversation in which each party has the opportunity to respond at their leisure and yet be assured of the other person's complete attention. There is no worry about waking someone up with an ill-timed phone call—lovers who cannot sleep can write e-mail at three A.M. without fearing that the other person will be inconvenienced.

For those who are married, e-mail offers much more privacy than telephone contact. There are no messages to be explained, and it is possible to put passwords on files to protect them from being read by unauthorized people, and to keep unauthorized people from retrieving and reading e-mail.

The nonintrusiveness of e-mail is a powerful attraction to the relationship itself. In today's industrialized society the frequency of communication creates a sense of being almost constantly intruded upon. Phone calls at work, pagers, cell phones even while driving, answering machines, television and radio commercials, ads in movie theaters—all constitute an ongoing barrage of intrusions into one's thoughts, privacy and enjoyment. Family members, too, have a way of being intrusive: Spouses and children demand attention, and not even bathing is safe from interruption. But an e-mail lover is *always* nonintrusive, always waiting for the convenient moment, never interrupting something else important or demanding attention that is already split five ways.

In this respect, it is certainly difficult for 3-D partners to compete with computer friends who never intrude. No matter how sensitive or thoughtful, a real-world companion must sometimes interrupt a bath, wake one from a sound sleep, or become unhappy and need comforting (frequently during the biggest game of the season!). For those who are married, the daily grind is intrusive—paying bills, doing laundry, making sure the kids get fed. All of these demands are miraculously absent from the e-mail relationship.

This idealized form of communication, never intrusive, never demanding, allows computer friends to become more attached to each other. The relationship moves easily from friendly mutual interest to feelings of being emotionally boosted. The rapid development of intimacy leads to a sense of needing each other, yet even here the computer relationship can prevent that need from becoming abrasive or off-putting. Fantasies about being together can cement a sense of attachment, and these feelings emerge as "falling in love."

QUESTIONS YOU SHOULD ASK

If you are involved in an online romance, you want to try to get as realistic an idea of what your Internet lover is like as soon as humanly possible. You need to gather negative as well as positive information. Try to notice the very subtle clues that can tell you about his or her personality and that suggest problems that might arise.

If you have not told anyone else about the romance, you should break away from that secrecy. Have a trusted friend read both sides of the correspondence for a while. First let your friend read your own messages, to get a feeling for what you are saying about yourself. Then ask your friend about the personality they see in your lover's messages to you. Get a few suggestions about hard questions you can ask your lover in future messages, questions that may help you decide whether to meet in person.

Here are some hard questions that you can ask your lover, to help you get a realistic picture of him or her:

1. **"Are you seeing anyone now?"** Although anybody can lie, it is a good idea to ask the other person directly if he is currently involved in another relationship. It's also a good idea to ask if he is involved in any other online relationships. If he is, be clear with yourself and with him about what that means about your own relationship.

2. **"How many online relationships have you had?"** If she has had dozens of powerful online relationships, you may be less likely to connect with her in person. You might ask her why those relationships ended (if they are over), and what happened if and when she met her lovers in person. Be prepared to discuss this topic yourself too—turnabout is fair play.

3. **"Why did your last relationship end?"** We all have bad

luck sometimes in relationships, but his explanation of why his last girlfriend is no longer in the picture is an important piece of information. What he says can tell you about his attitude toward women in general, and about what kind of problems he's had with the women in his life. If you have negative reactions to some of what he says, be up front about discussing them with him. If you develop reservations about the wisdom of this relationship, talk it over with a friend or a therapist before you go any further.

4. *"How many times have you been married?"* For those in their thirties and forties, this question can be an indicator of several things. Multiple marriages can mean that there is some real problem in the way she chooses men or relates to them. Again, multiple marriages isn't necessarily proof of some fatal flaw, but it's worth thinking about. On the other hand, if she has never been married, it isn't a bad idea to discuss the reasons for that as well. A person who's never been married by the age of forty may have a fear of commitment or, again, be choosing people who don't want a committed relationship. But whatever the reason, discussing it is an important avenue to understanding each other.

5. *"What would your ex tell me about you?"* This is a hard question to answer, because it's painful and because it's difficult to be completely honest. But I think it's a good springboard for a discussion of the problems that could not be solved in the previous marriage. A frank discussion of what would be different—and the same—in *this* relationship should follow. Tell your own story as well, and really try to look at the ways

that this present relationship is repeating successes and problems in previous relationships.

Other points of advice would include:

6. ***Get down to the nitty-gritty of everyday life.*** How often does he bathe? How clean does she keep the house, and what are the little things that drive her crazy? What kind of food does he eat—are you both vegetarians? What about her religious preference, church attendance, use of alcohol and drugs? *Ask outright.* Be very clear. Then talk over your feelings about the answers you get.

7. ***Ask for a reference.*** Is there someone out there you can talk to about your lover? Is there someone where you live or on the Internet who knows him in person? It may seem like an imposition to ask for this, but you are putting your heart and soul into this relationship, and on the Internet you can't meet her friends at a party, or his co-workers at the office, when you stop by to pick him up for lunch. So ask to "meet his friends."

If you don't have a trusted friend who could look over your e-mail messages, you may already be spending too much time on the Internet <g>. See a therapist who can go over both sides of this relationship with you.

IF YOU ARE MARRIED

Unless you *want* to have an extramarital affair, some safeguards may help you keep a level head in your Internet friendships. First, if you are keeping the relationship a secret from your spouse, get rid of the secrecy. Secrecy provides extra excitement in Internet relationships, but that same excitement can cause you to ignore signals that the relationship is getting out of hand. Tell your husband or wife about your Internet friend, and tell your Internet friend that you have done so— and that you might even let your spouse read the e-mail exchanges.

If you find you are already falling in love with this person you know only through the Internet, stop right now. End the Internet relationship and get marriage counseling. Talk to your minister, or sit down with your spouse and honestly talk about the problems you see in the marriage. Realistically, the longer you let the Internet affair continue, the more damage you are doing to your marriage.

If you feel you can't end the relationship and it has become too important to you, then I strongly recommend you seek individual psychotherapy. You need to explore the things that are happening in your life and in your marriage that make you vulnerable to this kind of relationship. At the very least, talk to a trusted friend—but not to one who thinks extramarital affairs are no big deal.

Don't meet the person, don't exchange phone calls and don't start having cybersex. Just as you avoid affairs in daily life, you must keep sexual activity out of the Internet relationship.

Finally, consider taking a break from Internet chat boards

and Usenet groups. If the majority of your personal contact is with the person on the Internet, you need to walk away from the computer and spend some time with your spouse. Take up a new activity that you can both enjoy, like square dancing or hiking or sailing. If you don't, you will find it harder to avoid having an Internet affair.

THAT FIRST MEETING FACE TO FACE

If you have decided that you are seriously interested in the other person and that you want to meet face to face, you may wonder how to go about it. Because the first meeting is such a significant experience, many Internet people have posted their ideas about how to arrange one. This posting[1] offers guidelines for the first offline meeting:

> In your online or telephone interactions with Mr. or Ms. Right, you don't have the same clues or inferences you do in 3-D. Online is a SPECTACULAR way to meet someone wonderful.
>
> When you decide to meet offline for the first time, it's very important that you let several people know about it. When that first meeting time comes, give that person's information (full name, User ID number, phone numbers, address, and some personal information about them) to several people you know and trust.
>
> When you know your plan to meet, set up a schedule with a couple of those friends to call them at a specific

time so you can check in and let them know you are okay. Then, **MAKE SURE YOU CALL WHEN YOU ARE SUPPOSED TO!** And advise them that if you don't call, something is wrong! They need to do what you have advised them (perhaps calling you where you have told them you will be—whatever your plan calls for).

Remember, better safe than sorry! I can't stress this enough. As many wonderful people as there are out there, there are a few that are not so wonderful. We need to be aware of that and protect ourselves.

Now, on to that first meeting!

The time has come!! You are going to actually **MEET** <sigh> Mr. or Ms. Right!! You are psyched!! This is the meeting of a lifetime! You've already practically ordered your tux or are thinking of baby names.

This is the time to take a **MAJOR** time out!

First-time meeting expectations can kill the best of relationships. Now is when you need to talk about the guidelines for that first meeting.

1.   Remember that you do get along. You are friends first!! You feel that there is potential for this relationship going the long haul. There is a real possibility that there may be no chemistry there. There may be no 3-D attraction. Be aware—and know that it's okay!! You are friends. You are friends first. That leads to number 2.

2. **Treat each other with respect.** Even though there may be some dashed hopes or hurt feelings, it's not intentional that that happened. It's a part of online life. (That's why it's soooo important that we keep a check on those expectations.)

3. **Enjoy your time together.** You had so much in common initially that even if you don't click, there is enough of a basis there for you to have a really good time together. It may not be what you were hoping for, but enjoy what you have.

4. **Be honest!** If you meet someone and you can tell they **ADORE** you, but, well, it just didn't happen for you—let them know. This is probably going to be one of the hardest online things you will ever have to do, but it has to be done. If you can't do it in 3-D or on the phone, at least send them e-mail. I've heard so many stories of people that thought it was all okay, only to never hear from that special person again. To have them never call, never return calls, not answer e-mail. This isn't fair to them. This is a person that you WANTED to meet. You had your own expectations. It didn't work. Again, it's okay. But closure for that other person is very important. It is the right thing to do.

5. **Have a contingency plan.** You may **NOT** get along at all. (Remember the story of the couple that met after spending so much time on the phone and online—and he walked off the plane looking like he hadn't washed his clothes in a month and had

never even **LOOKED** at a toothbrush?) **Plan an alternative course of action in case you wind up being alone—just in case.**

6. **Plan in advance what you are going to do. Make a map of your entire time to be spent together. Where will you go? What are you going to see? Have the entire time mapped out—and be prepared to alter that map as you go. If you really hit it off, you can go in any direction that you want. If you don't, at least you will still have had a nice visit, and hurt or hard feelings will hopefully be kept at a minimum.**

As for that first meeting, talk about it in advance. Talk about what will happen if you don't hit it off. Talk realistically about the situation. Be open with each other. Don't look at it with rose-colored glasses. Honesty is important—especially to yourself.

Although the loss of an Internet love is generally not as lastingly painful as the loss of an in-person love, the loss is still significant. The fantasies were seductive, the amount of time spent was probably enormous, and both of you were experiencing your attachment in the same way you would be attached to someone in ordinary life.

In the Reuters news piece at the beginning of this chapter, two people met on the Internet but never met in person until they were going to be married. I wish them well. For most people, making this kind of commitment is unthinkable without the physical meeting.

CHAPTER 4

Is It *Real* Love?

From: RainGoddess
To: Estherg
Subject: Real Love

I have fallen in love with a man I met on the Internet—at least, I think it's love. Can it be real love? I've never met him, but we exchange about 20 e-mails a day and spend hours on the phone. I've seen his photograph, and he really turns me on. Frankly, my heart just skips a beat when I see his name in my e-mail list. He seems to have everything I want in a man, and I think I love him. But it scares me—how can this be real love? Over the computer? Never having met? Do you think someone can fall in love like this?

THE QUESTION OF LOVE

Many years ago, one of my psychotherapy patients was preoccupied with the question of whether the feeling she had for her boyfriend was real love or just infatuation. We talked about this issue for months, reviewing her ideas of what love is and how she would know if her love was real or not. In the end, she could not come to a conclusion about it and decided that if she was that uncertain, she should try to find another relationship.

When I was a "consulting psychiatrist" to a chat board (that is, an active participant who happened to be a psychiatrist), I frequently received private messages from other participants who had questions about their relationships or who needed to talk to someone about disappointing or upsetting experiences in those relationships. One woman told me she had connected with a man on the chat board and that they had spent hundreds of hours talking, both on the board and on the phone, and had agreed to meet in person. She told me that she was seriously thinking of divorcing her husband to be with him.

After we had spent some time with her discussing whether her feelings for him were real love or not, she would frequently update me on the relationship. One night when I came online, she immediately sought me out to tell me that she had broken up with her boyfriend because she had caught him engaging in "hot chat" with other women on the board. Although she had talked to him about it, they could never resolve the conflict between her desire for an exclusive relationship and his belief that he was doing nothing wrong by having computer relationships with other women.

Now that I have been investigating the psychology of love between people who meet in cyberspace, the same question has arisen: Is this real love?

The answer is *yes*.

There is no doubt that the love people feel for others they meet via e-mail is some kind of real love. But I must caution here that just because the feeling is real does not mean that the relationship will turn out any better than a relationship with someone in 3-D life. Nor must every feeling of love necessarily lead to a real-life relationship.

The feelings of love that Internet people may have for each other fall into many categories. Some of them are passionate love, based on an early intimacy and enhanced by physical attraction upon meeting. Some are a kind of obsessive love, a preoccupation with and almost disabling focus upon the other person.

Some Internet lovers come to the conclusion that they love each other before they even meet or without ever meeting; others come to that conclusion after months of steady communication, visits across oceans and a real comprehension of each other's lives and personalities. Some have gone from the computer to the chapel without any intermediate stages, while some have left marriages of long standing to make a connection with someone they have known briefly but intensely over a computer chat board.

The problem with identifying real love is that we generally define it as love only in retrospect, after we know whether the relationship "went anywhere." That is, we are apt to define our feelings based on how the relationship turns out. If the romance is short lived or ends with storms and heartache, our psychological makeup tends to define those feelings retrospectively as an infatuation rather than as true love. But if we marry and live long together, then we feel we are really in love. The exception: Most people will define the feeling they have for their *current* lover as real love.[1] So when John asks himself if he can possibly really be in love with Starchild (chapter 3), the answer is likely to be yes.

HooperD, a twenty-five-year-old man in Tennessee, met AbleSusan, a twenty-two-year-old woman in Denmark, in a discussion of rock bands on the International Relay Channel. The first couple of times they interacted, she wasn't particularly impressed with him. She told him that she didn't like American men, they were too full of themselves and had little education worthy of the term and their thinking was muddy. Stung, HooperD responded by engaging in conversation with AbleSusan whenever he came across her in the board, determined to prove that he was smarter and more thoughtful than she assumed. Over the course of several nights, HooperD was successful in convincing AbleSusan that he was worth talking to.

Their chats soon became more personal, and they began to make dates to talk to each other in real time on the IRC. Every morning they would spend an hour (free of long-distance charges because the call to the Internet is a local call for them) writing back and forth to each other. They sent e-mail during the day, sometimes dozens of notes, anytime they thought of something worth saying or some new response to a previous letter. In spite of the time difference, their relationship flourished to the point that they talked on the phone. When HooperD had a vacation, he went to Europe, and toward the end of his trip, he went to Denmark to see what AbleSusan was really like.

Three months later AbleSusan joined HooperD in the United States, and they were married. The total time elapsed from meeting on the Internet to marriage was about six months; their actual time together before deciding to get married was less than ten days. Now when I run across HooperD on the Net, he tells me that things are going well and is even a bit surprised that I would wonder about it. He believes that he knew AbleSusan very well before they were married, better than he had known other women he had spent months dating in person.

If HooperD and AbleSusan divorce in the near future, they will likely decide that they had only been infatuated with each other. If I get invited to their tenth-anniversary celebration, we will all agree that this was indeed real love. If Circe and Cadet (chapter 2) finally crossed the ocean to meet and get married, they would tell us that their feelings for each other were real love.

Since poets and writers, psychologists and philosophers have all been unable to finally determine what exactly love is, I am not going to try to do that here. But it seems worthwhile to explore some ways of thinking about love and the kinds of love people experience, and how that love may show itself in computer relationships.

I believe that there is no difference between the feeling of love one has for an e-mail lover and the feeling of love one has for someone first met in person. Computer lovers feel the same kinds of warmth, yearning, anxiety and even obsession that are hallmarks of falling in love with anyone, in any situation. The differences here are in the styles of love. The balance of the erotic, intimate and commitment qualities of love is generally different in computer relationships from that in 3-D relationships.

WHEN SOULS MEET

Since Internet relationships based on exchanged e-mail messages are formed "from the inside out," the intimacy component is usually the most prominent. In those formed through cybersex connections, erotic qualities can be the most significant. In relationships formed in ordinary life, the first component for most couples is the erotic or passionate quality, while the formation of intimacy is much slower.

The experience of falling in love "across a crowded room" is usually one of an immediate erotic attraction. The information one can gain about a woman in a room full of people is limited: her appearance, perhaps a gesture or a toss of the head, a smile and the subliminal clues about social status drawn from clothing. Yet the experience of immediate attraction to a stranger across the room is not uncommon. Something similar happens across crowded chat rooms—but with much less information. A choice turn of phrase, a snappy comeback—and that one person stands out from all the others writing notes back and forth. But the erotic qualities perceived in person are not present on the Internet—the basis for attraction is intellectual or emotional rather than physical.

Even with cybersex, the attraction between two people is not an actual physical attraction. While they are exchanging sexually explicit fantasies, they are not reacting to the physical being of the other person—they are reacting to their writings. The intensity of the experience is based on an intellectual activity; the attraction is based on a meshing of fantasies without any awareness of each other's physical reality. Indeed, given that deception is common in cybersex situations, the actual appearance of the other person may turn out to be repellent, where the fantasy person fulfilled their wildest dreams of beauty.

In face-to-face relationships, intimacy can take quite a while to grow and may never be a working part of the relationship. Many relationships fail because the degree of trust, openness and communication is inadequate for intimacy. But intimacy is often the first component of a computer relationship and can arise very quickly in the early stages. This feeling of intimacy, of emotional closeness, combined with attachment, feels like love to many people.

In an e-mail relationship, information about negative attributes is often completely absent, allowing for a positive projection very similar to a feeling of love—even at the beginning, when there is little romantic interest. This positive projection does not always last: Many e-mail relationships collapse very rapidly when unacceptable personality traits become evident.

It is hard for love to develop if people hold significant political or philosophical differences. In forums specifically devoted to those subjects, these differences do become evident quite quickly. But in a photography forum, discussions about presidential races may come late or not at all, and in a Usenet group about heavy metal bands, it may be very difficult to find out that the other person holds beliefs about the environment diametrically opposed to yours. By the time you become aware of a major difference that would otherwise signal you to get out of the relationship, a deep attachment has been formed, and you may decide to ignore those differences.

Robert Sternberg, in his book *The Psychology of Love*,[2] talks about the components of love in a way that is very helpful to understanding Internet romances. He states that love can be thought of as having three basic components: intimacy, passion and commitment.

INTIMACY

Intimacy here means not sexual but emotional intimacy: the ability to reveal your innermost self, warts and all, to another person. Such emotional closeness and sharing of even negative feelings is one of the hallmarks of computer relationships. Most of the individuals involved in these relationships have a closeness and connectedness with their correspondent that is painfully missing from ordinary life. As with Cadet and Circe, the progression from general conversation to exchanges of deeply felt personal experiences and fragile fantasies can be rapid. Most of the people I've spoken to applaud this exchange of profoundly personal information—this intimacy.

Various aspects of computer relationships—the anonymity of the first interactions, the ability to reveal parts of yourself that you normally keep hidden—appear to promote intimacy. Writing out your thoughts to a faceless other person has the quality of writing in a diary, opening up to another person in a nonthreatening way. The simple act of writing allows for greater self-exploration, while presenting yourself in the best possible light increases the likelihood that you will experience your e-mail relationship as positive by comparison with other relationships.

Stallion met Lady Peace in a chat room devoted to the discussion of gender issues. Stallion, a twenty-seven-year-old single man, lived in Kentucky, while Lady Peace, a twenty-nine-year-old divorced woman, lived in Florida. Although they were frequently on opposite sides of debates, he found her to be a gentle person; her responses were reasoned, and she was kind even when disagreeing with a respondent. In the aftermath of a flame war, in which Lady Peace had held her own against attackers without ever seeming to lose her temper, Stallion wrote her privately to congratulate her on her forbearance and her good humor.

For a while they wrote back and forth in an idle way; Lady Peace was busy with a project and wasn't interested in devoting a great deal of time to the chat board. But when Stallion lost his job, Lady Peace became his main support and cheering section as he hunted for a new one. When he found a new job, their fantasy celebration included champagne and roses and ended with a goodnight kiss.

They began to write many times a day, and their letters were increasingly warm and even romantic. Their mutual fantasies were satisfying to both of them, and they began to feel that they were "in love" with each other. But they did not exchange photographs until some time after they decided they were in love, preferring to keep their relationship "soul to soul" for as long as possible.

Sharing the difficult time together had brought Stallion and Lady Peace closer. As the correspondence continued, Stallion shared his feelings about his work, his sense of losing himself as a person when he wasn't working, and his feelings about what it meant to be a man in this culture and how his work was tied in to those feelings. These discussions of difficult and even painful feelings, and their willingness to share even negative aspects of themselves with each other, is what made Stallion and Lady Peace more intimate.

Lady Peace also was able to write to Stallion about her feelings about him and what changed for her when he lost his

job. Not all of her feelings were positive, and some of the
things she told him about her feelings would have been off-
limits in many relationships. She had a sense of him as complaining rather than coping with his problems and told him
so. They exchanged hundreds of notes about themselves and
their feelings about each other, and as a result of sharing both
negative and positive information, they felt that they could
say anything and be heard. They felt love for each other.

In 3-D life truly close friends can experience this kind of
trust and intimacy. But my investigations found that many
people find this degree of closeness *only* with people they met
first through the Internet. Most of them agreed that a person's
physical reality in a face-to-face meeting restricts that intimacy and even slows down its development.

The frequency and speed of e-mail contact also enhances
intimacy. It is easy to tap out a quick note on the computer
about a sudden insight into a problem or a fight with your
boss. Experiences that would never rate a phone call are
transmitted with the speed of thought to an e-mail companion. If there's a double rainbow this afternoon outside your
office window, you can send a note to your friend and share
the enjoyment.

Most of the relationships I have explored have been
between very verbal and generally literate people. In a computer conversation, the ability to successfully communicate
thoughts, opinions and descriptions is generally the most highly visible aspect of a person. With all these factors, intense intimacy and then feelings of love may develop much more rapidly and easily on the Internet than in face-to-face encounters.

But intimacy by itself is not enough to create love. Some
kind of attraction (and some flirting) is necessary. The kinds
of unconscious personality attractions that are present in 3-D

relationships are also present in the early stages of computer relationships—but in a fairly unadulterated form.

The mutual attraction of personalities may create a bond of love and lead to erotic attraction, passion and commitment. But even with only the initial intimacy, Internet love can feel as strong as any love in a 3-D relationship.

PASSION

The second component of love that Sternberg identifies is passion. Passion can certainly be a part of an Internet relationship— as someone once said, our primary sexual organ is the brain. With "hot chat" and cybersex, and the sharing of romantic and sexual fantasies by e-mail, sexual attraction can be as powerful via computer as in daily life. But without meeting each other in person, without experiencing the physical "chemistry" that makes a relationship erotic, all the passion and eroticism are occurring in the form of transference, or the projection of daydreams and erotic fantasies onto the other person.

In face-to-face encounters with strangers, people do not always present themselves in the best light. Your hair may be soaking and makeup ruined from a rainstorm. You may trip on a rug or drop a tray of food. But such mishaps can't happen in a computer meeting. Even though you may be hanging around in your bathrobe or are in need of a shower, on the Internet you are as beautiful or as handsome as the other person imagines you to be.

The relationship between Circe and Cadet had a great deal of romantic fantasy—fantasy motorcycle rides through the Alaskan wilderness are romantic and even sexual. Without ever meeting in person, they had an erotic component to their relationship. For some people, an exchange of photographs begins their true physical attraction, if the pictures are found to be even a little attractive. But as we discovered between Wendy and Karl, even when the two people do *not* look the way they imagined each other in daydreams, the preexisting intimacy can bridge the emotional connection and the sexual or passionate connection. As in ordinary life, a foundation of trust and emotional closeness can spark a physical attraction.

From: Lady Peace
To: Stallion

My dear one, my beloved Stallion,

I know I have been putting off sending you a photograph, and I haven't looked at the one you sent me. My stomach knots up whenever I think about it, and I know you will think I have little faith. But I have come to think of you as my lover, without any idea of what you look like, and I'm afraid. What will happen to us if our physical selves don't mesh with the way our real selves have? What if you don't like the way I look? What if I don't like the way you look? Will our love survive or die an untimely death because of some flaw in our 3-D selves?

I'm afraid that I'll turn out to be a shallow person, or that you will. But when I read back over our notes, I know that you are not a shallow person, that your heart is with me, and I don't think I'm the kind of person who cannot look beyond the outer layer to the spirit—but I'm still

afraid to bring our bodies into this. Oh well, sometimes you just have to jump in and see what comes—my photograph is attached, and I'm going to look at yours right after I send it. Courage!

All my love—Lady Peace

Fortunately for Stallion and Lady Peace, the photographs generated a physical attraction, which only increased when they finally met in person.

In daily life, you may be attracted only to people with a particular type of body appearance, then fall in love with someone who looks nothing like your daydreams. Computer relationships can hold similar surprises in the development of love.

The experience of physical passion is how most people, in ordinary life, become aware that they are falling in love. When you see his face, your heart skips a beat. Her voice on the phone is exciting, raises your heart rate, is sexually arousing. When you are together, you can't keep from touching each other, and even the slightest touch can bring on a storm of desire.

E-mail couples feel some of these same sensations upon getting e-mail from their beloved: Their heart skips a beat, and they become excited. Touching is not possible except in fantasy, yet computer partners rely on physical sensations (to some degree) to alert them that they are falling in love. Fantasies of touching, kissing and holding can provide a tremendous degree of sexual arousal, and even without actual physical contact, the erotic attraction may feel very real. But in an Internet romance the attraction is to the imagined person, and not to the real physical person on the other end. This is the most significant difference between Internet relationships and 3-D relationships: the fact that sexual attraction is based only on fantasy. Even when photographs are exchanged, the actual sexual compatibility of two people who have been "lovers" for months is impossible to predict.

From: Moss
To: Estherg

Starchild told me you were a psychiatrist, and I wondered if you could help me here?

I have been writing to my boyfriend, Jim, for about three months now, and it's been really great. We can talk to each other for hours on the phone and have been having cybersex for about a month. I thought we were in love. But I went to meet him this week, and even though he's a pretty good-looking guy, seeing him in person was weird. I mean, when we talk on the phone or chat online, I get pretty aroused (I'm blushing here), but when I saw him, well, there wasn't anything. It wasn't like he was ugly or smelled bad or anything, but when we held hands, I just wanted to pull away.

I was planning to have sex with him when we got together (I know he was planning on it, too), but it just never happened. Now I feel really uncomfortable even writing to him. Do you have any idea what's going on with me? Is there something wrong with me?

The relationship between Moss and Jim had been based on their emotional connection through e-mail and on the phone, but the chemistry wasn't there when they met in person. Physical attraction seems to be based on many different factors—things like how a person smiles, or whether they have dimples, or how they smell (and not just whether they smell bad)—that can't be conveyed over the computer. In a computer relationship sexual fantasies provide all those missing components, but once you meet in 3-D reality forces you to deal with the person's actual physical characteristics.

Another factor with Moss and Jim is that they both were very anxious about the meeting, more than they were aware of. That level of anxiety can dampen physical response. Moss's fantasies of Jim may have been so strong and/or so unrealistic that the real Jim seemed like a stranger to her. The reason she didn't react to him was that she didn't "recognize" him. Possibly with enough meetings, in which Moss and Jim get to know each other and get used to each other, Moss will know if the potentiality for a physical attraction that matches the computer attraction exists.

But Moss now regards even her feelings of love for Jim with suspicion. Because the physical attraction was not there in person, she now doubts that she was ever "really in love" with him. Clearly, attraction of some kind is necessary for love. As long as they had not met, Moss's sexual fantasies about Jim were enough to make her think she was in love with him. When her sexual fantasies were destroyed by their personal meeting, her feelings no longer seemed "real."

COMMITMENT

The third aspect of love that Sternberg identifies is that of commitment. If it is difficult for people to find commitment in relationships in daily life, people in computer relationships have even greater hurdles to cross. Computer relationships tend to fall short in the area of commitment—possibly because of the evanescent quality of the e-mail communication itself.

Commitment has several different stages. In the earliest stage, the relationship is important and both people plan to continue it, spending time on it and treating it with a degree of respect. In 3-D life, this early-stage commitment calls for a couple to keep dates with each other and not to break them for trivial reasons. They return each other's phone calls and are willing to make at least short-term plans for future dates.

This early level of commitment is certainly available in e-mail relationships, although planning for and keeping dates is not really required. Early-stage commitment instead takes the form of a tacit agreement by both parties that they will respond promptly to each other's messages and plan for the relationship to continue. The commitment to keep dates does not come up until the couple is making arrangements to talk on the phone or to meet in person.

A deeper stage of commitment involves exclusivity, sacrifice and long-term planning. In a 3-D relationship, exclusivity means committing oneself to not see other people romantically. Sacrifice means that if you are having an emotional crisis, your partner will treat it as important enough to sacrifice some other activity in order to spend time with you. And long-term planning is the ability to assume that the other person will be present at important times in their life, at holidays and other special occasions—and that they can plan to take trips or do other projects together in the future.

In a computer relationship, this stage of commitment is tricky. Many people have multiple and simultaneous relationships on the Internet, and they often have little sense that multiplicity is wrong or unkind. But sometimes, too, the partners don't agree on exactly how exclusive their relationship is.

Since there have been divorce cases in which computer relationships have been cited as adulterous affairs, at least some people feel that a computer relationship has the same significance as any other extramarital affair. But for other people, the significance of the relationship is highly variable. Some view it as having the same quality and importance as a fantasy and therefore as no threat to any existing relationship in the 3-D world. Others feel that their computer relationship is as important and real as any other relationship in life.

Still, it is hard to commit oneself to a relationship via computer. Charles, a young man in London, had a long-term relationship with Zoe, who lived in New York. He was corresponding regularly with her, and had even begun to price plane tickets to New York to visit her, when she announced to him that she was dating a man she had met at a singles' party. He was shocked and hurt—he had considered himself unavailable for dates with other women because he was committed to Zoe. But Zoe apparently viewed her relationship with Charles as a side activity while she sought someone more geographically desirable, someone present in her real world whom she could see and touch.

The final stage of commitment is that of marriage, living together or buying a house together. At this level of commitment, a couple plans to spend their lives together, to mingle their finances and to formally take each other in sickness and in health, forsaking all others. Whether this commitment is enduring in the long run is less important here than whether the parties are willing to make such a commitment in the first place.

Some Internet relationships lead to marriage, so certainly some people on the Internet are able and willing to make this degree of commitment. But they are rare, because on the computer even the first two levels of commitment are difficult. This final stage of deep commitment is relatively unlikely without the personal contact, face-to-face meetings and dating that are involved in every 3-D relationship.

Still, marriages do result from Internet romance. Some couples do relocate across the country or around the world to be with each other. Clearly, these relationships have developed a significant degree of commitment—yet this degree is clearly rare. Most e-mail relationships run their course in about three months. Either the two parties meet and make a further connection, or the relationship simply fades away.

Is commitment required for real love? Judging from the many jokes on the subject, the deepest levels of commitment are not necessary for two people to feel that they are in love. But the absence of any commitment at all can end a relationship, regardless of how real the love may seem to be.

COMBINING THE COMPONENTS

The love that e-mail lovers feel for each other is real love, containing all three components of love. But in the balance of the three components, their relationships are somewhat skewed, which may explain why so many of these relationships are relatively brief. Although intimacy is evident, eroticism is frequently limited to fantasy, and commitment comes in at a distant third.

In ordinary life, the proportions are generally skewed toward physical attraction, at least in the beginning. Commitment in ordinary relationships is also greater than in computer relationships, probably because just getting together physically takes a degree of commitment not required for e-mail lovers.

But in ordinary relationships, intimacy, emotional sharing and willingness to deal with negative feelings all seem more difficult to reach than in computer relationships. Something about the possibility of being rejected by your real-world girlfriend hampers communication. One of the main problems I hear about in my practice is the difficulty of feeling safe enough to talk to husbands or wives about the deepest personal issues. Rejection by someone so close and physically present can be devastating. But safety is commonly one of the earliest and most satisfying aspects of computer relationships. A yearning for emotional closeness is one of the things that pull people toward computer romances.

Even though Internet love is "unbalanced" in terms of the components of love—the souls are entwined but the bodies are essentially uninvolved—it is still a powerful and real feeling. Although we place a high value on erotic attraction as a reason to get involved and stay involved, the relationships with strong intimacy and commitment components can be just as durable, and possibly more so.

MOVING FROM FANTASY TO REALITY

Transforming a relationship from fantasy to reality is very difficult. In the world of cyberspace, virtual relationships can be perfect: romantic and funny, without the extraneous garbage of daily life intruding into the daydream of love. But the actual meeting can bring reality into sharp focus. Negotiation is necessary where none was before. Where will we meet? Will you come here to Denver, or will I go to Indianapolis? What will we do together during the visit?

Once the meeting has taken place and a deeper commitment has been made, the real-world problems of moving the relationship forward are sometimes daunting. Jobs and money and children from previous marriages are suddenly real, concrete issues, where they were previously only topics of conversation. Between geographically divided couples, the question of relocation must arise. Although I have found a few instances where the man moved to join the woman, the statistics show the woman relocates more often.

One couple had a disastrous relocation. Their Internet correspondence had given her no warning that he—by her standards—was too meticulous, obsessive, exacting and excessively clean, coming from a household dominated by a compulsively orderly mother. Nor was he able to predict that she, by his standards, would turn out to be sloppy and disorganized. In addition, he tended to keep his emotions to himself in face-to-face interactions, while she was quite expressive, of anger as well as other emotions. When talking on the Internet, their minds had been perfectly in tune, but their 3-D selves were in constant conflict.[3]

BEFORE AND AFTER

Until two people live together, they cannot find out such important information about each other—and, as many newly married couples find, marriage is a whole new level of learning. Although many participants in e-mail romance discussion groups felt that their online relationships plumbed the depths of intimacy, they found that meeting each other in person, let alone going on to marriage, involved still-greater intimacy of the most ordinary kind.

Marriage almost always presents a change in a relationship, and here Internet relationships and 3-D relationships converge for the most part. The process of dating comes to an end, and the process of truly coming to know each other and rely on each other begins, whether the relationship began on the Internet, at work or through the singles ads in the local paper.

But one difference between computer relationships and dating relationships is significant here. A dating couple whose main interests together include dancing, listening to music or going to the movies can continue those activities after they move in together and get married. But if their primary activity together is writing letters to each other on the Internet, one of the most basic aspects of the relationship comes to a crashing halt. Most people who wrote letters during their courtship stop writing letters in person.

Suppose e-mail has allowed two people to develop intimate communication. What happens to that relationship when they are living together, no longer having the need or even the opportunity to write to each other? Internet couples may find that the easy intimacy of the e-mail relationship is not available once they are sharing a bathroom, a checkbook and a house. Even as a marriage increases the need for open communication, its importance simultaneously increases the risks of open communication.

What face-to-face couples have in their favor is practice in communicating, starting out from superficial conversation and moving (hopefully) into intimacy. But online lovers must move in the opposite direction—from intimacy to daily life. This transition often comes as a shock and may be one reason many online couples back off from a relationship right after a successful first meeting. The ease of conversation has been changed, and day-to-day realities are harder for those who met on the computer to deal with compared with those who first met face to face.

Although some marriages between those who met only briefly in person have clearly been successful, some real pitfalls await those who move quickly from e-mail to matrimony. Dating has its place in the progression of a relationship. In the dating part of most relationships, mutual (non-computer-related) interests are established and day-to-day communication skills are developed.

If the physical attraction is adequate (not even necessarily substantial) when a couple meets, this attraction in combination with e-mail intimacy can lead to a durable romantic relationship. As we have seen, a few computer relationships come to marriage without ever having a physical meeting. Historically, over the centuries, human beings dealt more or less successfully with arranged marriages between parties who have never met; so there must be room in the human experience for marriages between two people who have never met but have a lively interest in each other's mind.

IS MY LOVE REAL?

You may be asking yourself if your feelings for your e-mail partner are real. As with Moss, the erotic attraction you felt over the Internet may not have survived the transition to a face-to-face meeting. Or you may be trying to cope with feelings of love that are disrupting an existing relationship. Or you may be deeply attached to a person you have met on the Net but you suspect that he is a poor choice for a life partner. You may be thinking of getting married without ever having met in person.

There is no handy checklist I can recommend to test the solidity of your feelings of love. Your own emotions can tell you if you are in love or not; and the question of real love is generally settled in retrospect. But the following questions may help you to evaluate your Internet love and make good choices for yourself.

1. **Does this love meet my needs for intimacy, passion and commitment?** Have you explored all the areas that are important for *you*? Your own need for erotic attachment may be greater or lesser than your e-mail partner's, or your needs for commitment may be different.

2. **Is this a wise relationship?** If you are married or in another committed relationship, you need to understand what is drawing you into this e-mail romance. You should consider getting therapy before you make any drastic changes in your life or take any irreversible steps. If you are single, you still need to ask about the appropriateness of this relationship. Does it make sense to you to relocate to be with your lover in another city, or another country? Do you have enough in common to make being together in real life comfortable, possible and workable?

3. **Do I know enough about this person?** Have you fully discussed the important issues of relationship history, lifestyles and the realities of their life and yours? Have you any way of finding out about them from people around them? Not that I am recommending that you hire a private detective, but the possibility of deception exists in any new relationship. In computer relationships, you have few opportunities to find out about the person from mutual friends or co-workers.

4. **Do I know "negative" things about my lover?** Just because you like the same kind of music or share a fascination with old movies doesn't mean you have plumbed the depths of understanding each other. Did you follow up on any comments that gave you reservations about your e-mail partner?

5. **Have I asked about really ordinary things like hygiene, dietary preferences and usual activities?** If it is important to you that your lover share your political, religious or dietary preferences, or have similar ideas about how clean a house should be, then you need to ask directly.

Yes, you really can fall in love over the Internet. Whether it is wise love, or love that can survive for any length of time, is a different question. Moreover, the balance of the components of that love may be quite different. In fact, as we look at relationships that involve married people becoming involved in Internet affairs, and at pathological relationships, that balance may be very important.

CHAPTER 5

Electronic Adultery

SOMERVILLE, N.J.—A man filing for divorce accused his wife of carrying on a "virtual" affair via computer with a cybersex partner who called himself "The Weasel." Mrs. X's relationship with the man apparently never was consummated, but her husband claimed the pair had planned a real tryst at a New Hampshire bed and breakfast.

The husband filed divorce papers that included dozens of e-mail exchanges—some sexually explicit—between his wife and a married man she met on America Online.

The ease of e-mail communication leads to greater (and faster) intimacy. Most people find it easier to sit at the computer and write a note of any length than to write by hand. Composing a letter onscreen allows the writer to think, edit and send with minimal difficulty. There is no need to make several drafts, to cross out or to start over with a fresh page. No paper is necessary, no hunting for an envelope or a stamp, and you don't even have to walk to the mailbox. Unlike phone calls, there is no waiting for someone to pick up the phone, no need to leave a message on an answering machine and no problem with return calls coming when you are no longer available.

In my psychotherapy practice, I frequently suggest that patients keep a diary of some sort, to encourage introspection and to bring their thoughts and feelings into focus. Writing seems to be a helpful adjunct to talk therapy, allowing patients to spend time with their own thoughts outside the therapy setting. The very process of writing becomes a creative outlet for emotions that would otherwise be difficult to process. Participation in Internet forums on many subjects seems to have a similar effect. Using this opportunity to express your political opinions and personal experiences, even to provide cooking tips, can be therapeutic in the sense of increasing your awareness of your own internal world.

Many people spend hours online simply chatting with strangers just to have this creative and introspective experience. For them, writing is an end in itself. The very process of being creative is satisfying—and that satisfaction is intensified by the responses of the other discussion participants. Debate, argument, agreement, all in some way intensify and validate experiences, making traveling through cyberspace much more interesting than many other leisure activities.

These interactions are free of the ordinary social restrictions on what may be discussed. You may not feel comfortable talking with your wife or husband if you are struggling with boredom, self-doubt, doubts about the marriage or the relationship, or fantasies and dreams for the future. This emotionally loaded material can easily cause conflict within a marriage and so tends to be avoided.

But in computer relationships, these topics are much more

easily discussed. An online conversation with a stranger at the other end of the phone line—voiceless, shapeless, far away and unconnected to daily life—can be an opportunity to talk about *anything*. There is no emotional loading on these conversations. One woman observed that people online get "in their heads" and tell her things they would never think of telling her otherwise. It is truly a seductive force.

Even psychotherapy has limitations because the therapist is a living person, physically present in the room. The patient is consistently aware of this and so is always relating in some way to the therapist, regardless of the degree of introspection, regardless of their internal focus. People generally compose e-mail, however, in relationship to the written word, alone with their computer. The sense of the person to whom the e-mail will later be sent is not immediate, the way the presence of a living person is. Being alone with one's thoughts also opens the way for thoughts to arise that would be very difficult to express to another human being present in the room.

The process of projection encourages this easy intimacy. As John was writing to Starchild, he imagined her responses because he *could not see them*. As he imagined her responses, he supplied all the details that he would have liked to see there—understanding, empathy, concern, caring. The same conversation with Paula, his real-world wife, would have been fraught with danger. Would she understand? he wondered. She hadn't understood some things in the past. She might be upset or anxious if he told her he was fantasizing about quitting his job and going into business for himself. Their finances were entwined. Once when he had idly referred to this fantasy, Paula became very anxious and made him promise never to quit his job without talking with her about it first. She might think he was crazy if he told her his dream of becoming a composer. She might laugh at him, too, if he told her about some painful experience he'd never mentioned before.

BOREDOM IN MARRIAGE

Soon after I was first married, married people would ask me, "So is the honeymoon over?" Their assumption that problems could and would arise that soon was unsettling. But their own experience had shown them that the day-to-day closeness and responsibilities of marriage eventually wear away the energy of romantic love. In a good marriage, it is hopefully replaced with trust and a healthy independence—but there is no denying that honeymoons do come to an end eventually and are replaced with *something*.

Early in their Internet relationship, John and Starchild began to explore some painful experiences. He shared his childhood unhappiness with "not having a father," and he shared his disappointment in his present family situation— something he had never discussed with Paula because of his belief that she would be too deeply hurt, maybe hurt enough to end the marriage, leaving him the way his father had left.

John felt that nothing in his marriage could be changed, that there was no point to discussing with Paula things that she was not responsible for or that she had not been willing to change in the past. This sense of unchangeability in long-term relationships can close off many topics of conversation. But the more fluid relationships on the Internet have no such restrictions—change, if change is necessary, seems possible and even comfortable.

Many patients have told me that over the course of years

of marriage, their feeling of wonder and elation have gradually been replaced with a sense of comfort—and sometimes with boredom with the same old routine. The belief that the routine is unchangeable without causing a major emotional upheaval prevents them from addressing the problem directly with their husband or wife. Although some couples have been successful in working with couples' therapists to change a seemingly frozen situation, others have found that after a few months of change, they returned to the "rut" they were in before, or that their attempts to make changes were unsuccessful from the beginning.

For some couples, the time and energy that one partner devotes to the Internet widens an existing gulf. When a Boston-area man bought a program with nationwide addresses and phone numbers, his wife wondered whether he was searching for an old lover whom she resented. Thus she was upset when she awakened at midnight and found him in their computer room with the door closed. "There was no reason to have the door shut," she said. Though the computer screen was blank by the time she entered, she never asked, and he never explained, what he had been doing, leaving her with a "feeling of jealousy."[1]

Even good marriages, long-term marriages where both partners would describe themselves as happy, are susceptible to computer infatuations or love affairs. The seductive quality to e-mail relationships can be unexpected, and they may not be prepared to resist it. John did not start writing to Starchild because he was hoping to have an adulterous relationship with a woman on the Internet—he wrote to her as a possible friend, as someone pleasant to converse with and as someone who was lonely and wanted some connection.

When ordinary couples share their pain and their dreams,

it brings them closer together. Doing even ordinary activities together is necessary for closeness. Reading the newspapers, talking about the day's activities, even washing dishes side by side can all be opportunities for conversation and provide a sense of belonging. As has been said about child-rearing, it isn't just "quality" time that matters; *quantity* time matters as well. But when a married person spends more time with an Internet partner than with their husband or wife, they take that time away from the quantity time with their spouse.

For one woman, her husband's involvement with the Internet created such problems in their marriage. In evenings past they would sit together on the couch and "relax and read the newspaper. We might have a conversation about something one of us read. But now, it's hopeless. He's so involved with the computer in the evening that I just don't say anything to him."[2] In this case the problem was not an e-mail affair but simply the novelty and excitement of being on the Internet, lessening the amount of time the husband spent on ordinary closeness.

A new and exciting relationship can destroy a marriage that is facing boredom. You may feel that you already know everything there is to know about your husband, while the man you met on the Internet offers fascinating new revelations. Your wife may not share your interest in fly fishing, but the woman you met in the fly-fishing Usenet group will spend hours talking to you about the sport you love. You may find out new things about yourself as you bounce ideas back and forth with your e-mail partner. As you and your partner build fantasies together, you learn more about what you want in life, and you may become dissatisfied with your marriage.

MIDLIFE CRISIS

Stephanie Fletcher, author of the novel *E-Mail, A Love Story*,[3] worked as an advice columnist for an online service. Over the years of responding to requests for advice about e-mail relationships, she noted that many of the questioners were in their forties, trying to deal with their midlife transition. She suggests that people who have online affairs are people who would be likely to have an affair anyway, to buy a sports car or otherwise deal with their fears of losing their youth or of change in their marriage.

Although John was not yet in his middle years, he was feeling that his life was not going the way he had hoped. His marriage was not meeting needs that he had been unaware he had, and now he was responding to the possibility of having someone to meet those needs. Whenever a person, regardless of their life stage, becomes aware that their hopes for the future are not going to be fulfilled if they keep their present course, the possibility of an extramarital affair becomes significant.

John felt that if he explored his sexual fantasies with his wife, he would open himself up to further pain. In a long-term relationship, the signals about what can and cannot be talked about become fairly clear. Even if John's belief that Paula would be unable to tolerate and respond supportively to his fantasies was in error, he still might not be able to bring himself to discuss them with her. Whether his fear of her negative response in this very delicate area was accurate or not, it prevented him from raising the subject. In an e-mail correspondence, however, the possibility of rejection of his sexual fantasies was not nearly so terrifying. Starchild's approval was not as important to him as Paula's approval—and Starchild's rejection would not be as loaded.

CYBERSEX

Some bulletin boards or chat boards are specifically devoted to expressing sexual fantasies. Their underlying premises guarantee that one's inner erotic world will be accepted, even encouraged. They offer the possibility that your vivid fantasy life may somehow be *shared with another person,* even if you will never meet that person face to face.

The absence of social and physical information about the other person allows fantasies to be more complete. It is easy to project your favorite body type or personality trait onto the other person if you lack all such information. Both (or all) parties to this interaction participate actively in the creation of the fantasy sexual experience. As one man on the Internet said, "The imagination is inexhaustible and, so long as there is no physical object to relate to, it can invest the strongest passions in the flimsiest of dreams."

Because of the fantasy quality of the experience, cybersex can be "better" than physical sex with one's spouse or any other real person. The possibility of negative experience—due to impotence, ridicule, physical danger or disease transmission—is virtually nonexistent. In real-life sex, these physical restrictions can provoke anxiety in many people. Getting undressed in front of a stranger or trying to initiate sex with a spouse is often rife with anxiety, but such anxiety is not present in the virtual sex experience.

Cybersex may be intensified by the fact that in real-life sex, people don't necessarily share their sexual fantasies with their partners. Merely writing out a sexual fantasy can be an act more bold, or more "dirty," than anything they might consider doing in person. Within a marriage or other relationship, restrictions on socially acceptable behavior or personal inhibitions may prevent an individual from being satisfied sexually. For some, the very fact of seeing the words of their fantasy "in print" enhances their intensity.

SEXUAL ADDICTION

Cybersex definitely has an addictive potential. The frequency with which one can engage in it has no physical limit, unlike sex with real partners. The anticipation or feeling of "wanting" of the cybersex experience can build over the course of hours, and when relief from that anticipation comes, it can be significant.

The repeated experience of anxiety, anticipation and longing (or craving), followed by release, can create an addiction to alcohol, cigarettes, cocaine or heroin. In much the same way, sexual addiction can also happen (though not all therapists agree that "sexual addiction" even exists).

People can develop a "tolerance" to sexual experience, in much the same way that they develop a tolerance to amphetamines or alcohol. The first time you engage in a sexual fantasy on the Internet is likely to be very intense because of the novelty. Over time, the novelty wears off, leading some people to create new fantasies more extreme than they ever had before.

The ready availability of sexual talk on the Internet accommodates this need for even more frequent Internet activity. One may eventually be spending hours and hours every day on the Internet, on the chat boards, exchanging sexual fantasies with many different partners.

In contrast to real-world sex, cybersex may occur hundreds of times in an evening, with the corresponding anticipation/craving and release each time. People who smoke a pack of cigarettes a day smoke twenty times a day—and one of my patients who was addicted to both heroin and cigarettes said that one reason she had a much harder time quitting cigarettes was that she was smoking them so *frequently*.

Some of my patients have just as much difficulty stopping computer sex. They struggle to do other things in their households (and at work!), but their craving builds and they find themselves making excuses to "just check the e-mail," which results in a six-hour session on a sex chat line. One man starts participating in cybersex as soon as his wife goes to bed; he stays up until the wee hours of the morning having sexual interactions with multiple partners.

IS COMPUTER SEX ADULTERY?

There is considerable debate as to whether, among married people, cybersex constitutes true adultery or whether actual physical contact is required before sexual activity becomes adulterous. Since at least one divorce proceeding has been based on the premise that an online relationship did constitute adultery and had consequently harmed the marriage, one criterion for adultery might be whether the relationship is damaging or has the potential to damage the marital relationship.

John's relationship with Starchild began with innocent exchanges but progressed to the point that it was clearly becoming a danger to his marriage. "Fantasies are okay," said

John to himself, "I'm only having fantasies." But his loneliness within his marriage made him susceptible to falling in love with Starchild. His intimacy with her met a need that he hadn't even known he had.

If most of your energy is invested in your relationship with another person and you're not sharing it with your husband or wife, then you are hiding a part of who you really are.[4] If you are hiding who you really are, then you will likely feel lonely in your marriage. Clearly, John invested a great deal of himself in his relationship with Starchild, spending hours on the computer that were essentially stolen from his marriage. He might have recognized this investment as a sign that something was not working for him within his marriage, and he could have addressed that lack or that problem directly and possibly enhanced his marriage.

By not addressing the problem in his marriage, however, John and Paula grew further and further apart, until John took the step toward physical adultery: meeting Starchild in person.

If John was not seeking an adulterous relationship consciously, was he perhaps seeking one unconsciously? He would have described his marriage as a happy one, and he was not aware of wanting an affair, but he became involved in an online relationship anyway. Not everyone who participates in computer forums or discussion groups or Usenet groups becomes involved in an intimate relationship. Why did John?

The fact is that many people who have been married for years experience a decrease in their sense of mutual closeness. This fairly common phenomenon has been included in the broader "midlife crisis." Midlife crises are commonly associated with businessmen having affairs with their attractive secretaries, but men and women are equally susceptible to the experience of emotional emptiness and/or boredom within marriage, and they are equally susceptible to the experience of having someone "out there" think that they are wonderful, interesting, funny and sexy.

A fantasy life online can be exciting and stimulating, and as I have noted before, an online relationship is ideal in the sense of making no real demands, imposing no daily grind to deal with. These ideal qualities are also present in the first stages of face-to-face relationships: The lovers feel a renewed energy, may need less sleep, feel more important in the world and are completely absorbed in thoughts of each other. Their times together can seem idyllic—and they probably are. (As time goes by and they move in together or marry, the idyll comes to an end and real life begins.)

Computer affairs *seem* safer than physical affairs because they appear to be able to provide all that excitement and energy without threatening the marriage. John reassured himself on this point continually, even while he was escalating the computer relationship to a more real one, involving phone calls and, eventually, in-person contact. "I was very realistic in knowing that I had no intentions of giving up my marriage, and never wanted that. It is part of that twisted loyalty that I possess that caused me never to want to hurt my wife but allowed me to seek fulfillment with a stranger."

Some people may be able to keep a computer affair restricted to the computer. But for most people the cybersex becomes repetitive after a while, and the novelty of the relationship begins to fade. They become frustrated and bored and want to move to a new phase. That means phone calls and in-person contact.

This limitation on computer relationships explains why many people who are having exclusively online affairs engage in them with more than one partner. Frustration and boredom with one cyberlover may lead the person to finding another, and then another. As I mentioned, those who engage in cyber-sex frequently do so with multiple partners. The repetitious quality of the computer sex may also lead to the exploration of more and more unusual and extreme fantasy material.

Society has not yet determined rules for behavior within Internet relationships. Although the rules for most sexual relationships in ordinary life assume fidelity, on the Internet it seems possible to have as many virtual lovers as you are able to find—and judging from my research, many participants in e-mail affairs don't feel they are betraying their real-world marriage vows by having virtual lovers.

RAISING THE LEVEL OF MARITAL DISSATISFACTION

Although at least some divorces have resulted exclusively from computer relationships, most married people would feel that the greatest betrayal would be for their spouse to have actual physical sex outside the marriage. But even without actual sexual contact, online affairs can raise the level of dissatisfaction within a marriage—as it did for John D.

From: Warrior8
To: Starchild

Your ideas about moving to New York together are entirely wonderful. I feel lately as though one more day

of coming home to screaming kids and catching flack for everything I'm doing wrong will be the last day. My wife has taken to being angry with me for everything (so it seems), and I feel as though I cannot do anything that would please her. She's constantly on my case, nagging me as though I were a little kid myself. I bet she tells her friends that she has "three kids instead of two," like I've heard some women say about their husbands. And there is never any time for music—the television is constantly on, and no one here wants to hear what I'm working on. I don't think I'm being irresponsible, and I go to that damn job every day and get tortured by the boss and bring home my paycheck—boy, I'm on a roll today! Sorry about all the complaining. If I didn't have you to talk to, I don't know what I'd do.

Several important issues are described in this e-mail message. First, it is clear that the relationship between John and Paula is suffering. The anger in the household has increased, and it seems very likely that as John takes his positive self almost exclusively to his relationship with Starchild, Paula is feeling the change in the marriage. Second, he is telling Starchild the things he should be telling Paula. He doesn't seem to be talking to his wife about his dissatisfaction—he is sequestered with his computer, essentially having a "my wife doesn't understand me" conversation with Starchild.

In John's mind, throwing everything away and starting over, as in his fantasy journeys with Starchild, has become a serious possibility. As his fantasy life becomes more ideal and more satisfying than his real life, he has less patience with his real-world family. Although a conversation with Paula about his feelings would be painful and would definitely produce anxiety about the marriage, the lack of this conversation is effectively dooming the marriage to failure. Job dissatisfaction, marital dissatisfaction, his sense that his life is not working—all these things combine to make John's dependence on his online relationship with Starchild a danger to his real-world marriage.

From: Warrior8
To: Starchild

Had another fight with Paula today—this time she's mad at me because the computer service bills are so high. And she's right, of course, $400 for a month is way too much. I hadn't realized we've been spending that much time on the board. But it feels like everything I care about is there with you in North Carolina.

It is possible here to blame Starchild as well—carrying on like this with a married man. But once again, the relative anonymity of the virtual relationship plays a big part. Starchild does not know John as a real person, and Paula is as amorphous as a dream character. She may be giving herself the same kind of reassurances as John, that this is only a computer relationship. She may be telling herself that if his marriage is really falling apart, there is no harm in her waiting to see what happens. Maybe he would be having these problems even if she weren't involved; maybe they had always been there. In real-life extramarital affairs, people use these kinds of rationalizations all the time—but the online relationship offers Starchild much more room to deny the reality of John's marriage. It allows her even to deny the reality of John himself.

The fantasy world in which John and Starchild are living makes no provision for the emotional pain that a divorce would cost John, or its effect on his stepchildren or his wife. While it is possible that John's marriage was already on the rocks, and that his dissatisfaction with his life was already in the works, his relationship with Starchild is crystallizing that unhappiness and strengthening his belief that things at home are unworkable.

By expressing his unhappiness to Starchild instead of his wife, John virtually guarantees that no change will occur. By engaging in his most significant intimacy with a stranger in North Carolina, he ensures that his marriage will become increasingly empty and Paula increasingly angry as she struggles to process her sense of being abandoned.

From: Starchild
To: Warrior8

Oh, John. You sound so unhappy. I wish there was something I could do to comfort you. Isn't there anything you can do to make things better between yourself and Paula? Wouldn't she understand if you talked to her about how awful your job is and how miserable you have been feeling? Me, I'd just like to take you in my arms and hold you, stroke your hair and, ever so gently, kiss your forehead.

Starchild demonstrates here the "doublethink" for which humans seem to have a tremendous capacity. She can simultaneously offer him advice and empathy in his marriage, while suggesting that she would be a more comforting option. This is not a deliberate attempt to undermine the marriage, but is an unconscious process.

The exchanges of e-mail between John and Starchild that I have presented here are somewhat idealized. I have omitted any mention of steamy cybersex in which couples like them often engage, and we don't know if they're also engaging in phone sex. But just as taking the intimacy outside the marriage is damaging to the intimacy of the marriage, taking sexual satisfaction outside of the marriage can also damage the sexual side of the marriage.

Most computer affairs never reach the point of actual physical sex. This fact alone may make them ambivalent, possibly even mitigate their destructiveness. They may even provide some movement in a stagnant relationship, be it movement toward a new level of enjoyment, or movement toward a realization that the marriage is unworkable.

Writing e-mail can enhance self-awareness, increase introspection and help a person become aware of things they had never realized. Even in computer friendships that don't have sexual or romantic connotations, these communications can be eye-opening to the writer. But it is romance that fuels the relationship for John and Starchild, and their common fantasy of being together in an ideal situation is seductive in itself.

In itself, adultery is not an addiction. But addiction to the Internet can lead to adultery, can be part of computer relationships that turn into cybersex and can complicate our understanding of those relationships. In the next chapter, we will look at addiction to and obsession with Internet relationships.

CHAPTER 6

Obsession and Addiction

"Of all human failings, obsession is the most dangerous—and the silliest."

WOODY ALLEN, *Mighty Aphrodite*

Anyone who has ever received a $600 bill for Internet services can testify to the addictive potential of chat boards and surfing the Net. Even when the term *addiction* doesn't seem to apply, there is no denying that some people are obsessed with the Internet, obsessed with chatting with strangers across cyberspace.

The difference between obsession and addiction is hard to define. There is a tremendous gray area between the two, especially when we are talking about a behavior instead of a drug. Ordinarily I would use the term *addiction* to refer to a drug-related problem, and *obsession* for an intellectual or behavioral problem. But it is clear from the addiction literature that some people, in response to certain behaviors such as gambling, develop actual changes in brain chemistry. People who suffer from gambling addiction can tell you that their emotional response to gambling, and the withdrawal they suffer when they stop, are remarkably similar to physical and emotional responses to addictive drugs.

Obsession, on the other hand, is less a physical than an intellectual problem, although there are certainly life-destroying obsessions. In psychiatry, we would call obsession a neurotic problem. For the purpose of this discussion of Internet usage, I am going to use *addiction* to describe the kind that most closely resembles drug addiction and is destructive in the way that alcoholism and cocaine addiction are destructive. When talking about obsession, I am describing a psychological problem that can actually be helpful for some people.

Some people who use the Internet develop significant problems in other areas of their daily lives because they can't *make* themselves get off the computer. The progression from simply being interested to being completely obsessed can happen within days, even hours. Claire told me that she first signed on to America Online when she was ill; in that single first session, she became so obsessed with the chat board that she began to spend as much as six hours a day online, running up huge bills with the service. She focused all her attention on her America Online "friends," letting her housework slide, leaving her children unattended and even calling in sick to work to allow herself to spend more time on the chat lines.

Although she tried to decrease her usage, she was unable to tear herself away from the computer. She would plan to go online for "just a few minutes to check my e-mail," and then she would check into the chat room to see if anyone she knew was there. Hours later, she would still be on the board, absorbed in talking to people in Australia and England. When she did try to slow down her usage, she would get anxious and restless. Nothing seemed interesting, and she felt depressed. She even found herself thinking that life wasn't worth living if she couldn't get on the Internet. She even began to feel shaky when she stayed away "too long."

Claire and her husband began to have fights about the Internet bills. Each time she swore she would cut her usage, but then she would wake up in the middle of the night and secretly spend time on the chat board while her husband was sleeping. When she was at work, she thought about the Internet constantly, looking forward to going home so she could sign on. She looked for ways to access America Online from work; at one point, when she crashed the network while trying to install the connection software, she nearly lost her job.

Finally, in the aftermath of a marriage-threatening fight, Claire came to therapy. My recommendation to her was to remove the modem from her computer and work with a twelve-step group to relearn ways to live without America Online. Using self-hypnosis to control her anxiety, and with the help of a sponsor she found through the twelve-step program, she was able to stop her Internet usage. But two years later she is still unable to say for certain that she wouldn't overuse the Internet if the modem were reconnected. Much like a recovering alcoholic who can never again have "just one drink," Claire cannot trust herself to "just check the e-mail."

As a psychiatrist, I approached Claire's case as a fairly straightforward addiction. She had all the symptoms of true addiction—she was unable to limit her own usage, and she continued to use excessively even though it had already created problems for her. Threatened with losing her job and even her marriage, she continued to spend hours on the Internet. She spent too much money on it and neglected her responsibilities; and when she wasn't online, all her attention was focused on when she would be able to get online—that is, when she would be able to use the substance to which she was addicted.

Claire even had withdrawal symptoms when she cut back on her Internet usage, including anxiety and a sense of tremulousness, depression, hopelessness and a feeling that life was not worth living. And each time she gave in and returned to her obsession (even when she had promised herself she wouldn't), her sense of powerlessness increased.

Like an alcoholic, she tried to "drink socially" but kept finding herself on a binge. She tried to use her America Online account as her husband did—he just signed on, got his e-mail, and maybe spent an hour or so in the chat rooms when he had time. But he didn't spend more time than he could afford, and he rarely got beyond the minimum charge. But every time Claire signed on, she ended up spending far more time than she intended. She could not make herself use the service in a way that was not destructive to her life.

These are the classic symptoms of addiction. Even though the Internet is not a drug, people who use it extensively can have withdrawal symptoms. They can continue to log on, even in the face of the terrible problems it causes them.[1] Just as people abuse alcohol or cocaine, they can spend too much money and too much time, lose their job or end up divorced because of this addiction.

Dr. Ivan Goldberg, a New York psychopharmacologist, coined the term "Internet addiction disorder" originally as a parody of other substance-dependence disorders in the *Diagnostic and Statistical Manual of Mental Disorders*.[2] Dr. Goldberg suggests that Internet addiction is a symptom of some other underlying psychological disorder, but Dr. Kimberly Young, a psychologist who directs the Center for On-Line Addiction at the University of Pittsburgh, believes that Internet addiction is no less an addiction in its own right than alcoholism or compulsive gambling. Some experts estimate that two to three percent of the online community—about 200,000 of all consumers of Internet services—have serious Internet addictions.[3] The fact that there is actually a center to treat this kind of addiction speaks volumes about the frequency and severity of these problems.

Both Dr. Goldberg and Dr. Young agree that even though discontinuing Internet use causes no actual *physical* withdrawal, "for some people Internet use takes up so much time that it causes 'discomfort, and/or decreased occupational, academic, social, financial, psychological or physiological functioning.'" These symptoms are a hallmark component of the diagnosis of addiction.

According to Dr. Young, the heavy Internet users who are most likely to develop an addiction are "middle aged females and those (both men and women) who were currently unemployed."[4] The currently unemployed include individuals with disabilities that prevent them from working. Clearly, one of the factors that make a person more likely to develop an addiction to the Internet is lack of social contact—the kind of loneliness faced by people who are unemployed or homebound.

It is not clear why middle-aged women would be more likely to develop addictive Internet usage. The explanation is most likely a combination of several factors. Midlife crises affect both men and women, but since women are more commonly invested in communication than men, a woman who is in a midlife crisis, instead of buying a new and exciting red sports car, might seek a new and exciting form of communication. Statistically, women have more depression problems in midlife, and the Internet can have a tremendous appeal for depressed people.

Other therapists say that certain personality types are particularly likely to get drawn into Internet addiction. People who are already obsessive or have poor impulse control, and people who have previously been addicted to other things are most likely to suffer from the inability to stop using their modem. My own experience with patients supports this: Those who develop an Internet addiction are those who also have problems with their job or their spouse, or who are depressed or fearful. Because they want to escape their daily lives, it is easy for them to become obsessed or addicted to chat boards, cybersex and multi-user games.

But even people who haven't been clearly obsessive in the past and who haven't been having other problems can become obsessed (although this is much less common). The Internet provides a wide scope for obsession—it offers so many possibilities, from relationships to research to debate to role-playing games. When previously nonobsessive people become obsessed with the Internet, their preoccupation is likely to "run its course" without outside intervention.

People who have struggled with an eating disorder, with compulsive shopping or with gambling are also more likely to develop Internet addiction than people who have never had those kinds of problems. Recovering alcoholics and recovering drug addicts are more likely to struggle with Internet addiction. In fact, every computer service I have explored has areas devoted to twelve-steppers, including, ironically, twelve-step programs for computer addiction. The Internet can provide twenty-four-hour support for recovering alcoholics—but I find myself wondering if an Internet "meeting" for chat-board addicts isn't a little like having an Alcoholics Anonymous meeting in a bar.

Finally, some people simply enjoy the Internet more than most other activities. If a person prefers to spend time on the chat boards rather than watch television, the likely reason is that the Internet is more interesting. Interacting with people online is more involving than passively watching television; and playing role-playing games can be more absorbing than reading a novel. Participating in the creation of the story line and developing a character uses more mental energy and more creativity than watching any television series. The important difference between enjoyment and addiction is the destructive quality of addiction.

As of this writing, America Online has moved to a flat-rate fee system, which allows unlimited access for a single monthly fee. Other Internet providers are doing the same thing. I predict that this flat-rate system will make it harder for Internet addicts to tell when they are going overboard, and easier for them to conceal from themselves the degree to which they are dependent on the Internet.

MULTI-USER DUNGEONS

Many personal relationships spring from multi-user dungeons, generally referred to as MUDs, role-playing games that can involve hundreds of people and run for years. The name refers to Dungeons and Dragons, a role-playing game that was popular in the 1970s and 1980s. When the Internet became easily accessible, such games moved into cyberspace, allowing strangers to take on roles and essentially write a story involving other role-players.

Some people run their MUD games in a window alongside whatever else they are doing on the computer. Some college students become so absorbed in their game that they fail classes or flunk out of school entirely. The seduction of the role-playing game is exactly that: the opportunity to play a role and immerse oneself in it.

People who are lonely, depressed or bored with their daily life can find a role in a game that makes them feel popular or important. Playing this role can become more satisfying and more important than anything happening in the 3-D world. This is another form of obsession or addiction.

The problem with love in role-playing games is that although the feelings of love may be real, the beloved may *not* be real. One young man reported that he had at least five distinct personalities in his MUD groups, ranging from a passively listening type of character to an aggressively sexual character. He expressed a different part of himself in each persona—but no single one of them really represented his "true self," which was an amalgam of all the people he portrayed.[5]

As with all other connections on the Internet, the important emotional events are taking place in the mind of the reader; the reader constructs a fantasy image, and the relationship is happening not so much between the two participants as inside of each of them. Although role-playing allows for the expression of different parts of each person, it also allows for the development of purely fictional characters—and immersion in the role is a primary requirement of successful role-playing. Therefore, while the process of falling in love in a game can be very real and even powerful for the lovers, the real person behind the screen is not always involved.

THE INTERNET AND DEPRESSION

Apart from tendencies toward addiction, depression can also lead to excessive Internet use. Jonathan, a twenty-six-year-old man who responded to my Internet questionnaire, said that he had become addicted to the Internet and was still addicted.

He had been treated for depression in the past but hadn't had a lot of success with his treatment. While he was actively involved in therapy, he hadn't told his therapist much about his Internet usage. But he had discovered that while chatting with someone online or playing a multi-user game, he felt good.

Jonathan felt better while he was on the computer than he did at any other time in his day. So he naturally tried to stay online for as long as he could. When he couldn't afford to pay the bills from the Internet service, he "borrowed" a friend's account (without their permission) so he could continue. When he was on the board, he felt "taken out of" himself, interested in a way that he no longer felt interested in his daily life. When his day was flat and tasteless, he could step into a multi-user game and become the ever-cheerful dwarf he had chosen for his role. Playing the role of someone who enjoyed life continually and even flamboyantly, he forgot for a time that his own real life felt empty.

During the game in which Jonathan played the happy dwarf, he had begun an Internet romance, which had moved into private e-mail communication. Although he felt quite desperately in love with his e-mail partner, he felt that he had to continue playing the happy role he had developed for the game. He didn't know how to tell his partner that he was not usually happy, that he had attempted suicide in the past and was now only hanging on day to day. His role in the game and his romance had become his "only reasons to live."

For Jonathan, the Internet use that had originally lifted him out of depression had itself become a problem, one that made him more depressed. Just as cocaine addiction can temporarily lift a person out of depression, Internet addicts eventually find that the helpful aspects fall away, leaving them with worse depression than before—only now they have an addiction problem as well. Jonathan felt that an originally innocent game of role-playing had trapped him into perpetrating a deception. The romance had become so important that he didn't feel able to risk honesty and lose the relationship.

Depression can also make a married person vulnerable to an extramarital affair, for much the same reasons. Life is not going well, one's husband or wife is no longer emotionally available, taking risks within the relationship seems impossible—but this new Internet relationship offers excitement and respite from pain. Obsession with the online relationship fills every available moment and pushes out the painful depressive thoughts.

For some depressed people, the Internet can be a therapeutic experience. Getting away from depression through thinking about a new experience can be helpful, and Internet support groups for those who suffer from depression can even save lives. I have even recommended Internet support groups to some of my patients who find themselves suicidal and despairing at three A.M. But I caution them against getting dependent on the Internet, against substituting Internet friendships for friendships and relationships in real life.

OBSESSED WITH A RELATIONSHIP

Both on and off the Internet, obsessions with relationships are perhaps the most common type of obsession. One woman, whose handle was Starstruck, told me she was obsessed with her relationship with her online lover. Like an Internet addict, she spent too much time online, spent too much money on her online service and found herself experiencing great anxiety when she was away from the computer too long. But she wasn't addicted to or obsessed with the Internet itself as an escape from the difficult problems of daily life; she was preoccupied mentally and emotionally with the *relationship* she had made. Her interest in the man was more obsessive than addictive—she "stalked" him through the Internet.

Starstruck spent hours looking for her boyfriend on the Net; she sought out his postings in Usenet groups and repeatedly visited his Web site. She collected the writings and photographs he posted on the Internet, and she tracked down his home address and home phone number, also through the Internet. Her fantasies in daily life centered on accidental meetings with him and on a soulful fairy-tale love affair she might have with him. In the course of her online activities, she had been angrily rejected by him, and it was because of her misery around that rejection that she sought therapy.

She responded to one of my postings on a chat board and revealed that before she had connected to the Internet, she had had much the same kind of obsessional relationships with people in her daily life. For Starstruck, the Internet obsession was simply a continuation of her usual relationship pattern.

Many people who have broken up with a lover have had the experience of continuing to be obsessed with that person. One might drive by his house at night or casually drop by the café where he works. Or one might call her on the phone and hang up when she answers, think about her constantly and reread her old love letters or spend the evening crying over photographs of times together. This kind of obsession generally runs its course without outside intervention, but for some people it becomes a nightmare of stalking—and of self-hatred for their inability to stop.

Obsession on the Internet seems to be much the same as in real life, with one difference: In real-life obsessions, the real person is likely to have been involved in the relationship. Online obsessions are more likely to be with the imagined person, the person created in fantasy on the basis of very little real-world information. In this way, online obsessions are much like the obsessions people develop about movie stars or other prominent people.

OBSESSION OR ROMANCE?

In an Internet romance, it can be difficult to distinguish obsession from a true romantic attachment. For many, being in love can feel a lot like obsession, just as obsession can feel a lot like love. How can you tell if your relationship is an obsession or a romance?

In the case of Starstruck, her activities *around* the relationship are probably the best clue to the obsessive nature of her feelings. Her focus on her online lover was extreme; tracking down his writings and all the other information she could find about him took up more of her time and energy than actually communicating with him directly. A focus on outside information is the most significant factor in determining obsession.

This is not to say that spending time finding things out about one's online lover is always obsessive; it is a question of proportion. Some degree of obsession with a lover is a normal part of being in love. If you spend an evening wandering through cyberspace, dreaming of your lover and looking up him or her on Usenet groups and visiting their Web site, that doesn't constitute obsession. But if you are spending every

evening doing so, in addition to writing notes to your lover—
well, that's probably obsessive.

Addiction or obsession on either side of a relationship can
lead to major problems. In the next chapter, we will look at
some of the pathological relationships that can develop
through online connections.

Pathological Relationships

*It was a beautiful wedding. The bride was glorious in
white lace, and the groom was dashing in his tuxedo.
The two met on the Internet and fell in love. They met
and married—and it wasn't until after the wedding
that the bride discovered her groom was a woman.*

You may have heard a story like this one on your local
news, or stories about other terrible events that happen with
Internet relationships. It is a grim fact that among the friendly, interesting and kind people one meets in the world, there
are some unpleasant and even evil people who will do harm
when the opportunity presents itself. The Internet is not free
of these people. When we visit a strange city, we know to keep
a close hold on our valuables—but on the Internet we often
have a curious sense of safety, produced by anonymity and by
the fact that one is generally at home when online.

Some horror stories have made their way into the national news. After spending months engaging in sadomasochistic
cybersex, a woman was killed by her online "lover" (the term
is in quotes, because I have a hard time accepting that indi-

viduals exchanging violent sexual fantasies are lovers in the ordinary sense of the word).

The New York Times reported that a doctoral student at Columbia was charged with attacking a Barnard College student he had met online. After meeting her for dinner, he invited her to his apartment and sexually assaulted her, tied her up and tortured her for twenty hours. About a dozen people from across the country told police in Manhattan that they had exchanged e-mail with the man. None of the people had had threatening conversations with him, but some of them said his communications had been "strange."[1]

America Online reports that it has 7 million subscribers and handles 10 million e-mail messages every day. This cybercity of 7 million must have criminals and sexual deviants, con artists and people who suffer from mental illness, just as any actual city of 7 million would have.

Writer Jesse Kornbluth posed as a woman on America Online, then wrote an article for the Los Angeles Times.[2] He describes himself as not meaning any harm but admits that he found the opportunity to take on a new identity irresistible and tried on the female identity in order to be able to participate in conversations that were for women only. He journeyed through various chat rooms for both sexes: "The women, in the main, come to talk; the men, in the main, seem far more purposeful. The result is a mating dance so crude it's hard to believe the practitioners are grown-ups—the cyber prom kings claim their queens, drag them off to private rooms and achieve what passes here for bliss."

He had no difficulty passing himself as a woman on the chat board: "I had one of the most powerful revelations of my life. I didn't need to do anything special to become a believable woman, I just had to be intelligent and open and atten-

tive and empathetic—gender differences really didn't matter."
In the course of his pretense, Kornbluth fooled at least one
man into thinking that he was a woman.

Although Kornbluth clearly meant no harm, the same is
not true of everyone who pretends to be something they are
not. To keep adults out of chat rooms for young people,
America Online has set up systems to try to prevent adults
from posing as adolescents or children. *Try* is the operative
word here; without being able to see the person who is writing, it is very difficult to prevent adults from posing as children—and there are no controls that prevent men from posing as women, straights from posing as gay or married people
from posing as single.

John Kaufman, a San Francisco–based writer, had the
alarming experience of being stalked by a woman on the
Internet with whom he had had only the briefest of interactions.[3] Kaufman had posted a note on a local computer bulletin board about a program he wanted to sell. A woman
e-mailed him about the program, then met him briefly when
she came to his apartment to pick it up.

Afterward, she conducted a search of the Usenet, looked
at the posts that he had made in the past, and then sent him
e-mail commenting on posts he had made in newsgroups on
topics as far flung as Latin American politics and the weather
in the Shetland Islands. After a month, she sent Kaufman a
post that deeply unsettled him—a three-page letter that basically was a summary of his life. "She's pieced together the
puzzle of my life from Usenet," he wrote. "She knows my
mother was a concert pianist. She knows what I wanted to be
when I was growing up—all because of Usenet, from postings
and discussions I've had there. Here was a total stranger who
knew my cat's name."

Famous people have suffered from the attentions of stalkers for years. Rebecca Schaeffer, star of a television sitcom, was murdered by a stalker in 1989. David Letterman makes jokes about the woman who repeatedly breaks into his house, pretending to be his wife. A man scaled the wall of Madonna's house and threatened her life. Because these people are famous, and their names and faces are constantly in the public eye, it's hard for most people to imagine that stalkers would also become obsessed with ordinary people. But the Threat Assessment Group, a security consulting firm in Newport Beach, California, estimates that there are 200,000 stalkers in the United States, and only 17 percent of their victims are celebrities.[4] Clearly celebrities attract more than their share of crazed fans, but that leaves the remaining 83 percent of victims to ordinary nonstars.

With movie stars, fans know little about the real person behind the screen, and so they have fantasies about the star based on the characters portrayed in movies or television shows. Fans can become attached to movie stars, can fall in love with movie stars and can become obsessed with them. On the Internet, some of the same conditions that allow fans to become obsessed with movie stars exist for ordinary individuals. Because Internet communication invites projection and transference, and because the people writing messages have little information about each other, they easily project their fantasies and beliefs onto each other.

In daily life, few people besides celebrities come into contact with large numbers of people outside their work or home life. But Internet relationships, like stardom, can bring one into contact with thousands of unknown people. Messages posted may be read by hundreds or even thousands of strangers, bringing the writer into contact with many potential friends—and potential enemies. A note posted in a discussion forum may result in the author getting flamed. Another note might inadvertently induce an unstable person to believe that "he was talking just to me, sending secret messages of his love to me."

Although most stalkers, in ordinary life, are former partners or spouses of the victims, they can target almost anyone.[5] There are enough unstable or mentally ill individuals in the world that one can cross paths with them in any walk of life, in any ordinary activity. You may be in a class at school with someone who later becomes obsessed; or you may help a customer at work who becomes delusional. But a brief real-life contact is not likely to be powerful enough to allow for the development of an obsessive fantasy relationship.

In e-mail messages to an Indianapolis girl, a man from Indiana threatened to rape her, give her AIDS and "track down each and every member of your pathetic family." The girl, who was twelve years old, had met the man, who used the handle Mr. Bungle, in a teenage chat room.[6] The police who arrested the nineteen-year-old man reported that he seemed to be a "nice kid" who "couldn't terrorize a jackrabbit in person" but who found that the anonymity of the Internet allowed him to act out his aggressive impulses.

But enough horror stories—let's look at the just plain unpleasant or unfortunate connections that have occurred on the Internet.

CYBER DON JUAN

Sungoddess met Bearman on the computer chat lines. Sungoddess, a forty-year-old married woman, became deeply involved in her computer relationship with him. He told her he was forty-two and single, and he described himself as "tall, dark and handsome." Their relationship started with friendly private notes on the chat board, then progressed to e-mail as many as six times a day and live chat sessions that lasted until the wee hours of the morning. They talked on the phone and exchanged photographs, and soon Sungoddess fell in love with him.

She described her marriage as a marriage of convenience and said that it had lasted for years out of a need for mutual support and for lack of any better options. She found her relationship with Bearman to be much more supportive and intimate and sexually more interesting than anything that had happened with her husband in years. She decided to fly to meet him in his hometown of Dallas. She bought her plane tickets and made arrangements to meet him at a hotel near the airport.

Two days before she was to leave, Sungoddess was on the chat board, telling her friends excitedly about her plans to meet Bearman and possibly consummate their relationship. To her shock, another woman on the board related that she too had made plans to meet Bearman the following week— but had canceled when she discovered that Bearman had been having relationships with two other women on the board at the same time. Across the country, Bearman had been making dates with women to meet him and had sex with several of them. Only by comparing notes on the chat board did the women begin to understand the pattern of Bearman's relationships.

Sungoddess was devastated. She had even been preparing emotionally to leave her husband, but now she was suddenly confronted with the fact that Bearman was simply engaged in arranging a series of sexual trysts for himself.

This kind of predatory relationship turns out to be fairly common on the Internet. Warnings about cyber Don Juans can be helpful, but do not always prevent mishaps.

HOSTILITY AND VIOLENCE

It is very easy to misinterpret e-mail communication. Without the ordinary vocal inflections and visual clues that let a person know the emotional context of a message, individuals engaged in e-mail are more likely to misinterpret the communication according to their own fantasies.

For example, in the relationship between HillClimber and Angel-4, Angel-4 misinterpreted the intention of HillClimber's angry note in response to her posts. She interpreted the note as making a valid criticism of her own writings, when his real intention had been to belittle her.

EllaCon formed a very close relationship with Mr. Limpet, a man she met in a political discussion forum on the Internet. Over the course of months, they wrote each other frequently—sometimes she would receive fifteen messages from him in a day. Mr. Limpet's notes were increasingly romantic, and he began to sign off "love" and to tell her that her friendship was all that kept him sane. Ella, on the other hand, was deeply committed to her marriage and had no romantic thoughts toward him at all. When she confronted him with this fact, his notes to her escalated to thirty or forty a day, pleading with her to continue the relationship.

Ella became very uncomfortable with the increasing intensity of the notes, especially when their tone shifted from pleading to increasingly angry. Early on, she had become fond of him in a friendly way, but now she was becoming frightened. After asking several friends for advice, she wrote him a firm note ending the relationship and requesting that he not write to her anymore.

Three days later, Ella received nearly a hundred e-mails from individuals who had participated in the political discussion forum. Many forwarded to her a copy of the note that Mr. Limpet had posted, apparently to all 350 of the listed group participants. The note accused her of "cock-teasing" and "seducing men into her snares and leaving them cold." The note continued with bizarre charges that she was secretly recording the discussions for later use for some vague but ominous purpose.

In daily life, many people have had the experience of being the object of rumors that someone spreads about them. Unfortunately, on the Internet a person can be harassed when multiple messages are posted accusing the person of bad behavior or even illegal behavior. When hundreds or even thousands of messages are sent out so easily on the Internet, spreading rumors takes on a whole new intensity.

Ella reported this harassment to the sysop of the forum, and Mr. Limpet was dropped from the membership. The harassment stopped with the one final blowout of letters. But in other cases, the harassment escalates to the point that people cancel their membership in CompuServe or America Online to escape their harasser. Because an overwhelming amount of personal information is available to a skilled Internet researcher, some people have had to move, change phone numbers and in a very few cases even take on a new identity to escape harassment.

Could Ella have figured out sooner that Mr. Limpet was not a good person for her to be communicating with? Consider this relatively early exchange of e-mail:

From: Mr. Limpet
To: EllaCon

My dear Ella:

I am wondering if you are married. I am divorced, and it's been an ugly situation. My wife, a consummate bitch, took me for everything I had. I am living in a virtually empty apartment, with no hope of improving my situation in the future. Seems like all the women I have ever been involved with have taken more from my life than they ever put into it. Makes me think that women have more political power than men—just look at all the benefits that women get from the labor of men and then they want more. Women want to work at men's jobs, but then when the labor is too heavy, they get a man to do it. You can't stop a woman from taking a job just because it requires more strength than a woman would have—but then the men on the job end up doing their job and hers, too. All this "equal opportunity" crap is just that—women want their share and also some of the man's share.

Surely you, as a conservative, can see that the equal opportunity and affirmative action rules are promoting the interests of women and minorities over men? I notice in your last posting that you seemed to be in favor of affirmative action, and I can't believe that of you.

Mr. Limpet

Please understand, I am not saying here that conservative political beliefs are an indication of a potentially unbalanced person! But in this letter Mr. Limpet demonstrates his hostility toward women in several ways. He shows that he believes that they are actively seeking to take things away from men, and that all women are like the women he has been involved with, in their alleged predatory attitude toward him.

What someone says about their former spouse or former lovers can illustrate very well their attitudes toward the opposite sex. Even within a discussion of political issues, Mr. Limpet managed to convey the message that women take things from him that they have not earned. He makes it clear that he feels constantly embattled with women for his rightful due, whatever that is.

Given this information, EllaCon could have imagined that at some point in the future, Mr. Limpet would project those same attributes onto her. She could have thought, "If he thinks all women are trying to take things from men, he might start thinking that about me." A man who feels that he is constantly locked into combat with women to get what he needs might well begin to feel that way about her.

Mr. Limpet's increasingly frequent and intense e-mail is consistent with this combat mentality—he behaves as though he need only increase the energy on his side of the "fight," and he will win. Mr. Limpet does not notice that EllaCon is engaged in another activity entirely, that she is trying to conduct a friendship and not a romance.

In daily life, we all hear many people tell stories about their experiences with the opposite sex. Anyone who has spent an evening on a bad blind date can relate to EllaCon's experience with Mr. Limpet.

Most people have probably been involved in at least one

unfortunate or undesirable relationship and will likely talk about it. But if every anecdote a person tells about previous relationships is negative, and every reference to the opposite sex is negative or has an unchanging theme, bright red warning lights should come on—DANGER!

Computer relationships don't lend themselves to violent interactions, since the two parties are generally miles apart. But violence does erupt in some cases. Although it is hard to predict with certainty that a particular person will become violent, the best predictor is a previous history of violence. Whenever you are becoming involved in a new relationship, whether it be in real life or online, it is very important to be aware of irrational anger coming from your new friend, or any history of previous violent relationships or behavior. Violent activities and a criminal record of violence should raise the danger signal.

But how can you become aware of the past or present violence in a person's life? Obviously, most people are not going to advertise their violent behavior or criminal record, either in person or on the Internet. But if a person with whom you are corresponding seems to spend a great deal of time detailing their violent altercations with pedestrians, bicyclists and other drivers, you might take that as a warning that they would be violent in a close relationship. If they frequently express admiration of other people's violent behavior, that may be a clue that they are placing a dangerous degree of value on violence as a solution to conflict.

People who are regularly involved in flame wars in which they make physical threats and express violent fantasies toward other forum or chat board participants, are probably also potentially violent in person. I would differentiate here between a rude or nasty comment like "You are a consummate jackass" and a violent comment like "I'd like to beat your head down between your shoulders." Rudeness and insults don't constitute violence; it is descriptions of physical violence or actual threats of violence that are likely to be clues to future violent behavior.

While the young man in Indiana may well have seemed like a "nice kid" who "couldn't terrorize a jackrabbit in person," not everyone who is "violent" on the Internet creates that kind of false impression. And I'm not so sure that the Indiana man wasn't potentially violent in actuality. If you don't want violence in your relationships, you should avoid these individuals, both on the Internet and in your daily life.

DEPENDENT RELATIONSHIPS

While he was corresponding with Sweetie Pie, Stalwart received the following message:

From: Sweetie Pie
To: Stalwart

Hello, Stalwart.

What a great handle you have. It suggests strength, standing firm, defending your country and coming out four square for apple pie and mom. I like that in a man.

Boy, have I had a day! First my boss was a real pain this morning. He couldn't find anything around the office, had to

ask me for every little thing—"Where's my coffee cup? Where's the Smith account file? Where do you keep the extra toner for the copier?" I tell you, the man is helpless around the place. All these interruptions, and I'm trying to do a big project. I mean really! What does he expect from me?

He was behaving just like my old boyfriend, you remember, the one I split with in college? The guy couldn't seem to manage even the simplest of chores, put red stuff in the white laundry, couldn't seem to find the toilet brush— always asking me where things were, like Roseanne says, "like my uterus was a tracking device." He was such a wimp, couldn't make up his mind about things and always asking me for advice. What is it about men that makes them so incompetent about simple things? When I look at the movies, I see strong men who can make decisions and take care of their women, but when I meet men in real life, they seem—well, dependent.

Maybe I'll meet a guy like you, eh? Someone strong and capable and stalwart.

Take care,
Sweetie Pie

Although Sweetie Pie is looking for a man to take care of her, she makes it clear that she holds the sexist stereotype that men can't function without the help of a woman, that they can't find things, can't do ordinary household chores. She expects men to be "strong and silent," as in old Western movies, but in her experience they are weak and dependent, and she always has to take care of them as though they were children. Since another message to Stalwart about her experiences with men falls into this vein as well, she is probably actively collecting experiences with men that fit with her preexisting belief and support her stereotype.

Just because she has told two anecdotes about helpless men doesn't necessarily mean that she believes all men are helpless, but she also says quite clearly that she does believe that all the men in her life are like this. Warning signals should be coming on in Stalwart's head as he reads these posts from Sweetie Pie. If she continues with this same theme, Stalwart would be well advised to do a fast-fade out of Sweetie Pie's e-mail, unless he is also willing to be stereotyped this way.

These posts from Mr. Limpet and Sweetie Pie demonstrate very obviously the kinds of beliefs the senders hold about the opposite sex. But most senders' signals will likely be more subtle, and the problems they indicate won't be quite so obvious. Some character flaws and even pathologies such as paranoia, preoccupation with violence and criminal thinking may become apparent only after months of reading someone's posts.

Some problems are much harder to observe in e-mail relationships than in 3-D relationships. One example is intrusiveness or inadequate attention to interpersonal boundaries. If a new boyfriend or girlfriend made five phone calls in a single day just to chat, most people would start to feel a little wary. If they dropped by unexpectedly, showed up at the office or attended family activities or holiday functions uninvited, many people would back off, create distance or even split.

In relationships in the real world, excessive dependence shows up quickly, but it is much harder to notice in e-mail relationships until both parties are already deeply involved. An e-mail conversation consists of several messages back and forth, and daily contacts would ordinarily be multiple. It is hard to tell the difference between a lively interchange and an excessive interchange.

Some people like relationships that are extremely or excessively close (in psychiatry, we call them "enmeshed"), and they will not likely respond to intrusiveness with wariness. Others need a great deal of distance in their relationships and will respond to even small degrees of "intrusion" by becoming more distant. One man might immediately become angry at and distant from a woman who calls him at work even once; another woman will become sad if her boyfriend doesn't call her at least twice a day at work.

In ordinary life new relationships often involve a degree of obsession and enmeshment, and Internet relationships are much the same in this area. Couples who meet on the Internet may spend hours talking on the chat boards, then more hours writing e-mail back and forth. If they talk on the phone, they may spend as much time "together" as any 3-D couple who is dating and falling in love. In fact, between writing e-mail, reading the responses and making telephone contact, they may spend *more* time together. Internet couples who have continual access to their e-mail, either because they work at home or because they have Internet access at their office, can "talk" throughout the day in a way that ordinary couples cannot—and would not necessarily want to.

OBSESSION AND DEVOTION

As I pointed out in the previous chapter, obsession is more likely when real-world information does not intrude. Without realizing that the other partner may be very different from their fantasy ideal, a person can fall in love with the fantasy and get "carried away" with their emotions, becoming obsessed with their fantasy partner. In one sense, this obsession can become a kind of "mania," or obsessive love for a perhaps inappropriate person.

Such manias have been described in literature, and we see them sometimes in daily life. A man or woman may become intensely attracted to a person whose beliefs, political philosophy and lifestyle are the antithesis of their own. They may not even like the person in the ordinary sense, but their obsession and attraction to the person may be overwhelming. Even while fighting against the attraction, even against their own better judgment, they may nonetheless end up seeking out the person. Although the attraction in this situation is frequently purely erotic, a similar attachment can occur through written communication as well.

Such preoccupations may be even more likely on the Internet. As John Kaufman discovered, it is possible for an obsessed individual to gather significant amounts of information on another person, both through publicly posted messages in various Usenet groups, and through research (some of which is illegal) through Internet information services.

When DanielleG, a young English-speaking woman who worked as a graphic artist in Paris, began to post messages on a Usenet group devoted to modern art, she struck up an acquaintance with Kandinsky, a young Englishman who was a devotee of the Russian artist Wassily Kandinsky. As their conversations became more personal, DanielleG realized that Kandinsky's lifestyle was very different from her own. He appeared to be living a bohemian lifestyle of drugs and parties, using Internet access in a coffee shop to write to her and post Usenet messages. Her own life was one of comfortable routine, tidy and predictable. She could see that they were hopelessly unsuited for one another.

DanielleG's discussions of art with Kandinsky were intensely interesting to her, but so was the seductive quality of his e-mails. The differences between their lives had a flavor of forbidden fruit, and his flamboyantly individual ideas seemed very attractive to her. She began to have powerful fantasies of going to live with him in England. In reality, the idea of leaving her job and her family to live in essential poverty with Kandinsky was repellent to her, but her fantasies were powerful and sexual, and she found herself at a loss to explain to her friends why she was so preoccupied with him.

Many nights DanielleG swore she would not return to the computer, that she would stop writing to him, but hours later she would find herself at the keyboard, writing lengthy and sexually explicit e-mail. Even as she wondered if her e-mail was serving as a source of sexual excitement for Kandinsky's friends rather than being read just by him, she felt she couldn't stop herself from exploring her sexual fantasies with him.

Kandinsky sent her a photograph of himself, taken by another artist friend and scanned into the computer. It was an erotic photograph, not sexually explicit and yet seductive. She found herself looking at it a hundred times a day, caught up in a desire to be with him. She told herself repeatedly, "Don't be a fool—there is nothing in this relationship you want! You must be crazy to keep doing this!" but still she wrote e-mail to Kandinsky, and finally she bought a plane ticket to England to meet him.

The meeting began a torrid and tumultuous affair—in which DanielleG repeatedly found herself appalled by the way Kandinsky was living. His home was squalid and filthy, his habits were erratic at best—and yet she continued the affair

for over two years. He never pushed her to continue the relationship, but she sought him out again and again, yearning for
him and hating herself for yearning.

Finally, DanielleG met a man in Paris who was attractive to
her, and she was able to end her relationship with Kandinsky.
She says now that, had she met Kandinsky in a bistro or at a
party, she would probably never have taken a second look at
him, but her contact with him via the Internet created feelings
that were already very strong by the time she realized how
"ridiculous" it was for her to be involved with him.

There is probably no dependable way to avoid developing
this kind of attachment. If DanielleG had focused intensely on
the marked differences between her life and Kandinsky's, she
might have been more distant or avoided closer contact. But
the seductive quality of the e-mail relationship overwhelmed
her ordinarily good judgment about relationships. As she
says, "It was like being struck by a lightning bolt."

HERMITS ONLINE

People with an extreme need for distance in relationships may
be more prevalent online than in daily life; they may not even
be able to form friendships in the 3-D world. But on the
Internet, alone at home before their computer, they are able to
have some form of relationship with others. The stereotype of
the computer nerd who is unable to have a relationship in the
real world and so becomes obsessed with relationships in
cyberspace, has at least some component of reality.

People who, for one reason or another, have little other
social contact may find companionship on the Internet and
even form romantic relationships there. People who are afraid

to leave their homes (agoraphobic), fearful of social situations (social phobic), extremely uncomfortable with people or even just profoundly shy may use the Internet as their sole connection to the outer world.

Other Internet users may have no way to tell that the person they are writing to is housebound or has no connection to the world life apart from their modem. When PackerFan talks about his friends and their lively interest in football, those friends may be exclusively people on the Internet. His discussions of football games may be live, in the sense of being real-time Internet chats, but he could be sitting alone in his apartment, tapping away at a keyboard and drinking a lonely beer.

Xmantis had a six-month relationship with a woman he knew only as Tanya. He met her on a forum where participants were discussing their favorite TV shows, and he began chatting with her in real time on a chat board. Soon they wrote private e-mail, where they exchanged personal information. She wrote about her reading, her friends and her favorite activities—which included skiing and hiking.

After a brief time, Xmantis began to feel quite attracted to Tanya, and over the course of two months, their correspondence went from romantic to sexual. He talked to her on the phone, and her voice was gorgeous. He later told me, "Just the sound of her voice was enough to send me over the edge." When they exchanged photographs, Tanya looked as good to him as she sounded. Xmantis said, "I was just crazy about her, thought about her all the time. She didn't live that far away, I could drive there in just a few hours. I wanted to meet her, and I began to think that maybe I had found a woman I could spend my life with."

A single man, Xmantis suggested to Tanya that they meet, and she agreed. They even chatted about their ideal wedding, and Xmantis had fantasies of walking down the aisle with this wonderful woman. But whenever they would make a specific plan to meet, at the last minute she would call him and cancel because of some work-related emergency. Xmantis began to feel that maybe Tanya wasn't being strictly honest with him. Was she actually married? Or so involved with her work that she didn't have time for a relationship? But if she was, then how did she spend so much time on the Internet, in hour-long conversations?

After two months of canceled meetings, Xmantis questioned Tanya about her avoidance. She finally revealed that she wanted to meet him but was unable to tolerate the anxiety that the idea of meeting him caused in her. Every time she arranged to meet him, she would become so anxious that she couldn't eat or sleep. From the time she made the date, she would be sick until she canceled it. In fact, Tanya told him, she worked from her home because she couldn't tolerate being around people at all. Because of her profound social phobias, she hadn't gone hiking in years or skiing since she was a child.

Xmantis was completely floored by this revelation. He had pictured Tanya as an active, busy woman with friends and interests like his own. Now he had to come to grips with quite a different reality. When he talked to me about this relationship, he became very sad and tears came to his eyes. "I really loved her," he said, "but there was no way for us to meet, and even if she could manage to meet me, how could we go on from there? She was virtually housebound, barely able to tolerate seeing the mailman come up the steps, much less go out to dinner or go skiing."

After a few more months of correspondence, their relationship ground to a halt. He still sees her on the forums and boards at times and chats with her in a friendly way, but he finds it painful and tends to avoid their old "meeting places," just as he would have avoided the real-world coffee shop that he associated with a painful previous relationship in 3-D.

Xmantis and Tanya would probably never have had a relationship in ordinary life, because they would never have met. They might have connected in a telephone call for some reason, and certainly relationships have been formed because of telephone attractions to a beautiful voice. But the likelihood that people this socially isolated will connect is generally very small, and without the Internet to provide the opportunity for her to connect with the larger world, Tanya and Xmantis would almost certainly never have crossed paths.

Tanya was somewhat deceptive in this relationship as well. Although Xmantis was quite honest and clear about who he was in the world, Tanya skewed her responses to portray herself as active. She talked about real-world friends, but those friendships dated from the years before her problems became severe. Her current friends were all on the Internet. She truthfully reported that she was interested in skiing and hiking—but deliberately did not mention that she had been unable to enjoy these activities since childhood. Wanting very badly to be a "normal person," she presented herself on the Internet as just that, carefully avoiding anything that would reveal her as anxious, isolated or unable to conduct a 3-D relationship.

Tanya's deception was certainly not intended as a mean thing, or to "con" someone into a relationship. She wanted desperately to live the life she described having, and she wanted to be in love with Xmantis and have that normal life of her dreams—but she could not.

DAILY DECEPTION

Other kinds of deception—more deliberate and less innocent—are also prevalent on the Internet. As one respondent
pointed out to me, everyone he runs across on the Internet is
handsome, tall, in good shape and exercises regularly. Well-
muscled men and women with large breasts seem to throng to
the cybersex networks. Some people conceal their real appearance, their real job and their real problems from their Internet
lover until the last possible moment.

Certainly people also engage in this kind of deception in
the personal ads and in computer dating questionnaires. But
since their intention is to meet in person—and soon—there's
a limit to the degree of deception that is workable. It's very
hard to maintain in an ad that you are six foot eight, when
your blind date will immediately notice that you're only five
foot six. If you portray yourself as rich or famous, it won't
take long for that lie to be discovered.

In *E-Mail, A Love Story*, Stephanie Fletcher relates the
story of a woman college student who formed a very powerful
romantic attachment to a man she met on a chat board.
Although she was somewhat honest with him about being overweight, she understated her degree of overweight. After months
of correspondence, they agreed to meet, and at the meeting
place she waited for him to drive up. When he saw her, he
burned rubber racing away from the meeting. Following this
painful and even vicious rejection, the young woman became
despondent and required psychiatric treatment.

This fictional account strikes very close to the reality of
some Internet relationships. The mean-spirited quality of the
man's rejection may be somewhat overstated, though I have

certainly heard stories that rival this one. Even people who are not "shallow" or preoccupied with physical beauty may receive a tremendous shock when their Internet romantic interest turns out to be hundreds of pounds heavier or otherwise markedly different than advertised.

Other physical attributes are exaggerated on the chat boards, some of them rather private <g>. In an ordinary relationship, maintaining such fantasies is just not possible. Many of my Internet pals are quite sure that the meeting of souls is more important than the meetings of bodies, but the physical reality of those bodies eventually matters.

Other deceptions involve financial status, personal status, social class, marital status and even gender. A woman who used the handle Sex Kitten told me of meeting Big Hunk in a cybersex forum. They engaged in computer sex, then telephone sex, and she was eager to meet him in person. In addition to the sexual connection, she felt he was really a friend and might turn out to be long-term-relationship material.

Big Hunk had told Sex Kitten he was wealthy, with two houses in California and a Mercedes, and he related stories of playing the stock market with tremendous success. He offered to pay her way to visit him, and it was only when the real moment came to make the arrangements that she began to wonder whether he was telling the truth about himself. Somehow the plane ticket never came, the meeting never occurred and he faded from the chat board.

Although Sex Kitten hadn't particularly been looking for a wealthy man to have a relationship with, she found it appealing to think that he would pay her way to see him. Her fantasy was that his social status made it more likely that he would turn out to be okay and not somehow impaired. But now she wonders whether anything he told her was truthful.

Since she had been honest about herself, it had never occurred to her that he would be deceptive with her.

On the Internet, in the absence of real-world information, deception is extremely easy. In ordinary life, a woman may tell her boyfriend that she has a high-level job, but when he calls her at work, it will be pretty clear that she is really the receptionist. If he says he owns a Mercedes, reality will make itself known when he always drives up in an old junker.

If she says she isn't married, but a man answers the phone when you call and she is never willing to have you come to her house, something is pretty clearly not on the up-and-up. This is especially the case if, in the background, you hear the sounds of children, or a man's voice leads to a hasty conclusion to the phone call. If you find your boyfriend waiting tables at a restaurant you decide to try, it seems unlikely that he really is an investment banker. It isn't that deception doesn't occur in daily life; it is just easier to detect than on the Internet.

Because the Internet allows for more deception, deception in general is likely to be more common among relationships that are begun there. It is more likely that an Internet romance, rather than a 3-D romance, will involve a person who is socially isolated and uncomfortable. And just as in daily life, the possibility of connecting with the wrong person always exists.

CAN YOU SPOT DECEPTION?

If you are getting involved with someone on the Internet, there are some things you can do to try (the operative word here is *try*) to establish their truthfulness. Check on her real name and phone number through directory assistance for her city. Multiple search engines are available on the Internet that can also help establish true information. If your Internet friend says he works at a particular place, you might check to see if he really does. Perhaps you have a friend in his city who could "check him out" for you. If none of these ideas pan out, you could ask him for a reference online, someone who knows him and would be willing to talk to you. Obviously, you would take the online reference with a grain of salt, but it's worth a try.

If you are so deeply involved with your Internet lover that you are planning to meet him, you should take the same kind of precautions that you would with a personal ad. You should pass all the information you have on to a close friend, arrange to meet in a public place and be sure to have transportation out of that place in case of disaster. Take steps to keep yourself safe, and remember that there is never any guarantee of safety. Some people have had private detectives check out their Internet lovers. I don't know if I would recommend this or not, but if you are considering flying to New York or London to meet him or her, it is an option.

DEALING WITH INTERNET STALKERS

I wish I could recommend some surefire ways to avoid Internet stalkers, but I don't know of any. Random interaction with strangers will always expose you to the risk of crossing paths with someone who has severe emotional or psychological problems.

But a few suggestions may be helpful if you do find yourself being stalked on the Internet. First, avoid all contact with that person. Don't send him or her any more e-mail, not even e-mail that pleads for an end to the relationship. Keep a record (and hard copies) of all previous e-mail, and if the person tracks down your phone number and/or address, get a restraining order immediately. Report harassing phone calls to the police and to the phone company.

Get an unlisted phone number, and terminate all your e-mail connections. If you sign up or with another online service, use another name. If you use your own name, there are multiple ways for people to find you on the Web. Notify your new service of the harassment, and make sure everyone in your household who uses your Internet address is clearly aware of what is going on.

Do a search for yourself on the Internet, and see how many ways you can get your own address and phone number. Then write to each server asking that your name be removed. To prevent being restored to the Internet lists when the next update happens, unlist your address in your local phone directory.

If the stalker pursues you beyond the Internet, call your local police department and follow their advice and procedures for self-protection.

Obviously, the Internet is not the only place where people get hooked into pathological relationships. If you have problems with finding healthy relationships in daily life, you will likely have them on the Internet as well. But healthy or pathological, relationships that arise on the Internet are not restricted to chat boards or Usenet groups. Sometimes, as we will see in chapter 8, they develop in the most usual place of all—work.

CHAPTER 8

Work and Love

At its corporate headquarters in Hong Kong, a multi-national corporation has a computer on every desk. Computers are networked to connect the corporate offices in Hong Kong to satellite offices around the globe. Mary Chen can send e-mail about her current project to her counterpart in Sydney and receive e-mail from co-workers in Los Angeles. Her offices connect through the Internet, and Internet research is a part of her job. Since the beginning of the year, she has been working intensely on a project with Sam Jones in New York; his e-mail to her fills her screen every morning with project information and lately with jokes and personal commentary on the day's events.

Although she has never met Sam, Mary has started to look forward to his notes and "saves up" jokes for him. She thinks of clever comebacks to his comments and tells him about the office gossip. Mary looked Sam up in the company directory and thought his picture was quite appealing—and told him so. Now she spends more of her time answering his e-mail than she really should, and she feels a bit guilty about the personal

*quality that their messages are starting to develop. But
the warmth between them is one of the highlights of her
day, and the increasing sense of attachment she feels
seems to be echoed by Sam on his end.*

*Lately, Mary has begun to ponder how she might
be able to meet Sam—and she looks forward to the
time when their mutual project might require them to
meet in person. She counts up her frequent flyer miles
and thinks about spending them on a trip to New
York. There must be some reason she needs to visit the
New York office. . . .*

Mary and Sam's Internet relationship is much the same as
other relationships described in this book. They have never
met, yet their e-mail connection has slowly increased their
intimacy and mutual attachment. For these two, the process
has been subtle and somewhat insidious; they didn't begin
their relationship deliberately. Like the other couples, Mary
and Sam share a mutual interest, only Mary's connection with
Sam was a work-related project. They were "assigned" to
each other.

The potential for developing a close relationship through
e-mail applies to work relationships as much as to general conversation on the Internet. Although there have always been
office flirtations between co-workers who interact frequently in
person or by phone, e-mail has enlarged the circle of possibilities
and has allowed the flirtations to go further. E-mail can also give
the illusion of greater privacy than telephone contact.

There are some differences between workplace Internet
relationships and other Internet relationships. First, the relationship may take a much longer time to develop online than
nonwork relationships, where the movement from discussing

a common interest to more personal and then more intimate writing can be very rapid. In fact, outside the workplace, the personal quality of day-to-day e-mail is present immediately, because the purpose and setting of the contact between the writers are entirely personal. In the workplace, however, most of the e-mail is clearly work-related: memos about meetings, notes about procedure changes, questions about inventory or plans for future advertising campaigns.

At work, the movement from very goal-directed e-mail to more personal interaction can be slow, and it generally requires an ongoing correspondence (often work-related). Your shared projects or interconnecting department concerns may require you to correspond with your co-worker for months or even years before you begin to develop a sense of relationship. It may just be a friendship at first, and the friendship may then progress to a romantic relationship.

In fact, it is quite common for workplace friendships to develop through e-mail connections. You might receive a joke (there are often several at any given time) that seems worth sharing with your co-workers. Or Harry in information services might attach a bit of gossip to a memo about a database to Joan in human resources. Passing on a joke, making a sarcastic or witty comment about the boss's memo or forwarding some especially boneheaded suggestion to a friend in another department, all move the e-mail connection into a more personal realm.

From: Harry in Information Services
To: Joan in Human Resources

Hello, Joan,

Got your last memo on the database problem, and we are looking into it here. I won't have an answer for you on that one for at least a week—best give me two weeks to debug what we come up with.

How's your new boss working out? I hear he's quite the pretty boy, definitely Brooks Brothers and button downs. Is he going to loosen up, do you think? Hope the day is going well for you—we've got chaos down here.

Harry

From: Joan in Human Resources
To: Harry in Information Services

Hi, Harry.

Gotta be careful with that Brooks Brothers stuff—I think I caught him reading your last note over my shoulder. Wouldn't want the feathers ruffled . . . He'll probably do okay, although I think that establishing a new dress code first thing on coming into the department is a poor way

to connect to your fellow workers. We'll just have to see.
So everybody in the company already knows about his
propensity for fine clothes (his and mine, I guess)—what
a grapevine! And you the biggest grape on it! <g>

Two weeks is fine with the database problem; we won't
be trying to use the whole package until next month anyway; the darned thing is definitely not user-friendly. User-
mugging, maybe.

So what's up with the chaos? Having a bad day? Tell me
more.

Joan

Joan and Harry never see each other on their large corporate campus, yet they form a community of co-workers and feel
themselves to be friends based solely on the e-mail they regularly exchange. It may seem remarkable that regular correspondents working at the same corporate facility might never
meet, but it is not all that uncommon for departments to exist
that are virtually freestanding; only department heads go to
meetings at the main office, and the employees who work for
them never come into contact with the employees in other
departments—except through the computer network.

In companies with multiple locations, employees may
communicate through e-mail exclusively. In fact, e-mail is in
some ways a key to making a multisite corporation into a uni-
fied company. At all the locations, the workers "know" each
other and can communicate easily. Gossip makes the rounds
through a grapevine routed through computer screens. As

Joan and Harry's correspondence shows, it is easy to move from purely business-related conversation to more personal and humorous commentary. Although the topics are primarily about office politics and the quality of their day, the interactions are friendly and even warm. If asked they would view themselves as being friends.

When Susan down in engineering breaks up with her boyfriend, Joan adds a sympathetic comment to a routine e-mail message to her about a policy change. Harry gets the word from Joan that Susan is having a hard time, and since he has been exchanging work-related e-mail with Susan for over a year, he drops his own sympathetic note to her. He also writes about his own experience with a recent separation, which increases the intimacy between the two of them.

From: Harry in Information Services
To: Susan in Engineering

Hello, Susan,

My boss is on my back about the new phone setup. What's the timeline on the changes in the cabling system that we need? Hate to bug you about it . . .

I hear from Joan that you're having a hard time of it this week. Let me offer myself as a shoulder to cry on—God knows I've cried on a few shoulders myself this past year.

When Carrie and I split up, I could hardly put two words together to make a thought. Work was nearly impossible.

I was just overwhelmed and would bend every available ear with my obsessing about what went wrong. I know they got sick of hearing about it down here.

I'm doing better now, thank goodness, and though it may be hard to believe right now, you'll do better again, too. Anything I can do, let me know.

Harry

Sharing sympathy about your co-worker's personal problem and relating your own personal experience to it is part of what changes a business relationship into one dealing with business *and* personal matters.

From: Susan in Engineering
To: Harry in Information Services

Harry:

Thanks for the kind words. It's been a real nightmare for me this past week; Jeff moved out and took pretty much everything in the house. I came home from work last Friday and he must have pulled up a moving van the minute I left for work; you can't imagine the shock! The place just echoes, and I have no idea what I'm going to do for furniture for the next couple of months. He also ran up the phone bill, and it turns out he hadn't paid the bills that were his share, so I'm really going to be broke for a

while. At least I'm able to be angry about it—if he hadn't been such a jerk about it, I probably would be feeling a whole lot worse.

I heard that you and Carrie split up, and now I'm feeling bad I didn't write to you and extend a friendly hand. You've got a cup of coffee coming from me; charge the latte to my account (oops, maybe I'll have to MAKE you a cup of coffee instead—finances, you know). How long did it take you to start feeling normal again? Right now, I could use a light at the end of this lonely tunnel.

Susan

In one e-mail, Harry has moved his relationship with Susan from a vaguely friendly working connection to a more intimate and warm interaction. He offers her sympathy and a shoulder to cry on, and Susan responds with personal details of her breakup. She tells him about her feelings—"I'm able to be angry about it" and "now I'm feeling bad"—and opens the door for more e-mail on the subject of Harry's breakup.

Susan has developed the idea that Harry is a warm and caring person, possibly more caring than she is. Her previous image of him, as a "geek" computer guy in information services, has changed and taken on a whole new facet. Harry gains in stature in Susan's eyes because of his apparent compassion for her, especially when she compares kindhearted Harry with the now-absent Jeff the Jerk, as she has taken to calling him.

For his part, Harry has the opportunity to daydream about having coffee with Susan. He may respond to her financial problems by offering to buy her a cup of coffee, or he may offer to buy her lunch. He may see himself as a knight in shining armor, at least partly because *he felt like one while writing his e-mail* to Susan, amplified by her warm and rather grateful response. Depending on how seductive this feeling is to Harry, he may feel more drawn to her. If he likes the feeling of being a knight in shining armor, his friendly feelings toward Susan can shift to an attraction for Susan.

The actual experience of writing e-mail has a considerable impact on the developing relationship. As Harry writes, he has an image of himself that he is trying to incorporate into this message. He feels that he is doing a "good thing" by writing to Susan, a feeling made more vivid by seeing his own words on the computer screen. As commonly happens, his feelings intensify because he understands them better, having put them into writing.

Harry and Susan have not met in person. They work in widely separated parts of the company and have had no reason to make a personal connection. They eat in separate cafeterias, and although their two departments work together continually, only the department heads or project coordinators have been meeting face to face. As in other computer relationships, this lack of information provides them with an opportunity to have daydreams about each other.

It is not an opportunity that Harry has in everyday life. Because he and Susan have not met, Harry is able to select a part of himself, a facet of his personality to present to Susan, without extraneous factors entering in. His sympathetic side is the only part that is being expressed as "Harry"; it is the only part that Susan sees. On e-mail, he consciously chooses to omit allusions to anything that might suggest self-interest or other background emotions. Had they met in person,

Harry's body language, facial expression, even eye movements would have provided Susan with a great deal of information about those background emotions.

Reading his own e-mail, Harry gains an image of himself that is more positive than the one he experiences in daily life; is it any wonder that when he is "with Susan," he feels better about himself than usual? It is a feeling that translates very easily to the kind of feeling that can lead to the romantic feeling of a 3-D date.

There are some restrictions on the fantasies that Harry and Susan can have about each other. They both know for sure that the other works at the same company and are quite clear about the job each of them has. Unlike e-mail relationships on the general Internet, possibilities for significant deception are absent in workplace e-mail relationships. In this respect, Harry and Susan have more reason to be trusting of each other.

Both Harry and Susan also have mutual connections throughout the company. Although they don't know each other personally, they do know people in each other's departments. A little conversation would enable each of them to get a reliable physical description and some friendly commentary on the other's personality, character and skill level. Again, this connection enhances their ability to trust each other in a way that people in ordinary computer relationships cannot. Most participants in online relationships have no way of checking each other's job or marital status, physical appearance or even the gender, but couples in workplace relationships do.

Even when an online romance develops between employees at two different companies who have occasion to exchange e-mail, much information about each other is available and dependable. Real names, real locations and real jobs are all readily apparent. It may be more difficult to track down the marital status of a fellow working at another company than someone in one's own company, but it can be done more easily than for some anonymous individual on the Internet. Moreover, handles and addresses used in the workplace are more likely to be straightforward, with less room for both symbolism and deception.

Still, even workplace relationships have considerable anonymity. Since Harry and Susan don't see each other, their images of each other are still essentially constructs. They don't have a physical sense of who the other person is, as they would if they saw each other every day. Susan is a vegetarian, and she likes to wear ethnic fabrics. When she is working on a project, she tends to chew on pencils—so that her desk always looks as though mice were feeding there. Harry has no pocket protector and is far from the stereotypical computer geek. He competes in the company tennis tournament and rides a motorcycle to work; and he is deeply involved in several long-running practical-joke wars.

Had Harry and Susan worked in the same office, they might never have formed an emotional connection, since the opinions that they had already formed about each other might have prevented Harry from making his offer of sympathy. Susan might have formed an opinion that Harry was "too much like Jeff" or "not my type," effectively precluding any deeper relationship.

As I said earlier, e-mail gives a greater sense of privacy than do telephone conversations. This sense of privacy made it easier for Harry and Susan to discuss their personal issues without feeling that a co-worker would be listening in. Let's take a look at the privacy issue.

PRIVACY IS AN *ILLUSION*

You may feel that your boss is constantly looking over your shoulder, and it may well be true. But in corporations all over the world, the boss is more likely to be looking over your e-mail. No matter how private a workplace e-mail system feels, the reality is almost certainly quite different. Corporate e-mail accounts are regularly recorded and saved—and quite often spot-checked by employers. In fact, it is now standard for companies to record all e-mail automatically.

E-mail sent on company time is actually considered company property, and the courts have *not* upheld the right of individuals within a company to send "private" e-mail. The private exchange of e-mail between individuals within a company has already cost fortunes in lost lawsuits. Racist jokes and sexist comments about co-workers can be recorded for all to read later—and very publicly in court. Small asides tacked onto workplace e-mail about business issues are not quite so funny when they are read into the court records.

Still, some e-mail lovers who use the company network to write back and forth spend hours on company time; some companies with Internet connections have found that employees are chatting live with friends around the world—at company expense.

Sophia, a young woman living in Paris, was deeply attached to her new cyberboyfriend, Joseph, who worked for a company based in New York. His corporate Internet access allowed them to write back and forth live. He constructed what he thought was a private e-mail access system, with a "room" in which he and Sophia could chat without the company looking in. Their relationship was intense and intimate. So it was quite a shock when one day, in their private "room," Joseph found a message from his boss saying that he had been reading the whole interchange and that it was now ended. Joseph lost his job, and within hours of the discovery of his illegal use of company equipment, he was escorted from the building.

In some widely publicized lawsuits, information that was casually sent by e-mail has later been used to prove sexual harassment and illegal practices. When one woman believed she had been fired because she spurned her manager's sexual advances, she hired John Jessen, "an electronic data detective."[1] Going through the company's e-mail, Jessen found this message: "I don't care what it takes. Fire the tight-assed bitch." Other kinds of e-mail can get an employee into trouble: bashing the boss, letting company secrets float around the Internet or leaking information to the press.

Even if you think you have deleted the e-mail, automatic copies were likely already made. A variety of software tools are available that can retrieve deleted data, even e-mail that was stored on disk and then erased. Jessen relates a story about an attorney who believed his computer security system was a match for anyone. He challenged Jessen to find anything that could be seen as damaging and then "watched in horror as Jessen dove into the system and pulled up old love notes from the lawyer to a former office manager." With e-mail, nothing is really private, and there is no real safety.

THE ABSENCE OF THE PHYSICAL

Todd has been having a problem with his immediate boss, June. When they are in a meeting together, he ends up frustrated and angry almost every time. Finally, one of his co-workers points out to him that every time Todd makes a suggestion, June contradicts him; but a few moments later, when anyone else in the room makes the same suggestion, it meets with June's approval. Conflicts between Todd and June have been going on for months, and Todd cannot think of any way to improve the situation.

One day Todd gets an e-mail from June about a problem with a project schedule. When he replies to her via e-mail, his suggestion is warmly, even enthusiastically received. Todd notices that what happens in e-mail exchanges with June is different from what happens in person with June. Whatever problem exists between them in face-to-face interactions is absent from their e-mail communication.

The cause of the problems in Todd's relationship with June became apparent when he met June's ex-boyfriend: Todd's physical resemblance to the ex-boyfriend was extraordinary. Most likely, June has been unconsciously projecting her very mixed feelings about her ex-boyfriend onto Todd because of their physical resemblance.

But in the absence of physical contact, June is able to interact with Todd easily, the way she does with other employees. Their e-mail connection is free of her confused feelings about him. When this lightbulb came on in his head, Todd vowed to minimize his physical contact with June for the foreseeable future and communicate with her as much as possible by e-mail.

Aside from the issue of Internet romance, many people find office e-mail to be freeing. In the neutral zone on the Internet, gender conflicts between co-workers are lessened. Diversity problems can be virtually absent, since skin color, physical disability and accents all are smoothed out in the anonymous world of e-mail. A man who is very uncomfortable when his gay male co-worker sits next to him in meetings may not be aware of the cause of his discomfort, but he can be much calmer when communicating with the same man via e-mail. Freedom from physical presence can ease such interpersonal anxieties.

On the other hand, the lack of physical presence can create problems for exactly the same reasons. At Pacific Gas and Electric (PG&E) in San Francisco, e-mail was "put to the test" several years ago.[2] When gay and lesbian employees marched in the city's gay pride parade, the company photographed the group's truck in front of its Market Street headquarters. "The incident prompted an electronic free-for-all discussion about homosexuality. Some antigay employees . . . aimed offensive messages at gay and lesbian colleagues." Although some were reprimanded for this behavior, "the reaction demonstrated a serious downside of electronic communication. E-mail is becoming our most prevalent workplace hate crime."

As we have seen, the anonymity of electronic communication makes flaming possible. Without face-to-face social conventions—without even a healthy fear of getting punched in the nose—e-mail writers can give way to saying things on the Internet that they would *never* say in person. Its faceless quality makes it easier to say hateful or racist things because the recipient is an essentially imaginary person. Even in companies, where handles are not used and anonymity is reduced, the person at the other end of the e-mail may seem much less real than they would at the other end of a telephone.

Most likely, none of the PG&E employees would have made hateful or antigay or racist comments to their co-workers in person or even on the phone. The reality of the other person even in a phone call is much greater than in an e-mail communication. Even when the recipient is clearly identified in the e-mail, the writer can feel as alone as when writing in a diary, and curiously safe from repercussions.

This sense of safety and anonymity is essential to many cyberspace interactions. Exchanging sexual fantasies, revealing deep personal vulnerabilities and reveling in socially unacceptable ideas all presuppose that the writer feels safe and anonymous. Even within the workplace, e-mail carries for many that same sense of safety.

Some people are using e-mail to create a paper trail to document their interactions (positive and negative) or to cover themselves in case of future problems. They send copies to everybody they can think of and hope for the best. Some people rely so heavily on e-mail that they lose sight of the need for any personal interaction at all, often e-mailing things that should be handled in person.

Another hallmark of e-mail is the difficulty of communicating background emotional color. Without the voice tones that accompany verbal conversation, a remark that would be made gently in person can seem rude or abrupt in e-mail. Based on the written content alone, a witty comment on e-mail can come across as angry, hateful or sarcastic. Although the intent of the communications in the PG&E case seems unmistakable, in the ordinary comings and goings of the workplace, some e-mail comments that would have been clearly understood as witty or even friendly in person are interpreted as angry and sarcastic.

Spoken language is greatly modulated by tone, body language, facial expression and even place. At lunch, the comment "Well, *duh*!" made by a co-worker about your blinding revelation can elicit a peal of laughter. The same comment over e-mail can be felt as critical or even nasty. (I find myself wondering if the same thing ever happens in a positive direction: Do people intend a message to communicate rudeness or sarcasm, only to have them seem positive or supportive when stripped of the sneer in the voice and the gleam in the eye?)

As a practical matter, I would suggest that you be very aware of the content of the e-mails you send in your workplace. Try to imagine what would happen if your supervisor were to read that comment on her clothing, or if you were one day to read your e-mail on the front page of the local newspaper? Just how would that somewhat sexist or racist joke sound in court, or at your next performance evaluation?

Always remember that as an employee, you are using company time and company equipment to send and receive e-mails. If your company has a policy about this (and most do), you should find out what it is and follow it—or start polishing up your résumé.

THE LONELINESS OF THE LONG-DISTANCE CORPORATION

Within big companies and multinational corporations, many employees are moved from site to site, packing up their families and belongings and moving to a new city. The faces of their coworkers change; grocery stores are unfamiliar; every facet of daily life shifts repeatedly. The only constant factor is working for Giganto Company. One friend who worked for IBM used to joke that the initials stood for I've Been Moved. At one party I attended, a prize was given for the person who had been moved the most times during their career—the record that night was eighteen times in twelve years.

Some companies discourage their upwardly mobile employees from forming connections within the community, so as to decrease their attachment to people and things out-side the corporation and thereby make transfers easier. Facing this corporate attitude, many skilled employees find them-selves lonely and isolated even within a workplace that employs hundreds. For these workers, e-mail can and does provide a stable network of companionship.

Such loneliness and instability can actually promote an e-mail romance. If you are lonely and isolated in your job, you're likely to be vulnerable to allowing e-mail to escalate a friendship into romance. When your stablest relationships are found through e-mail, it's not surprising that some of those relationships blossom into romance.

Even when employees meet in person and become friends in person, when they know what each other looks like and have some idea about each other's personality and character-istics, e-mail can allow them to deepen and intensify their relationship at a distance, providing a safe venue for the exchange of intimate information. E-mail can also allow shy people to converse more easily and enhance the emotional connection between two people who do not find each other physically attractive.

When the emotional intensity generated by e-mail commu-nication is combined with the necessity for out-of-town meet-ings, a potentially explosive situation is created. Carla, a mar-ried woman, was flying regularly to St. Paul, Minnesota, to attend project meetings for her company. She would be out of town three days a week, coming home on weekends and then flying off again on Tuesday. She stayed in a hotel in St. Paul, and generally at the end of the day, she went back to her lone-ly hotel room, wondering what to do with herself. Over the course of several months, she became friends with Sam, a man on the local project team, and they began to have dinner every night she was in town.

Increasingly distant from her husband, and cut off from her friends and companions, Carla found herself growing more and more attached to Sam. When she wasn't in St. Paul, she wrote extensive e-mail to him, partly about the project they were working on and partly friendly, personal messages. When the company decided to relocate Carla to St. Paul permanently, her marriage did not survive the move—but her relationship with Sam did.

Carla's attachment to Sam was based solely on her loneliness and lack of other resources. But the loneliness and work-related travel definitely contributed to her need to attach to someone. Her opportunity to exchange e-mail on a regular basis with Sam increased their mutual attachment, allowing them to maintain frequent contact even when Carla was not in St. Paul. The experience of writing to each other was satisfying in the same ways that other Internet couples experience—and the romantic aspects of the relationship were enhanced by the act of writing.

Why didn't Carla's relationship with her husband improve or strengthen through e-mail, too? Actually, in this case, Carla's husband didn't have much access to e-mail. But other established couples have said that their connection through e-mail *did* improve their relationship. Couples who live together, however, are much more likely to call each other on the phone than to exchange e-mail, unless their particular e-mail connection is easier or more convenient.

Established couples who communicate through e-mail have many of the same experiences as anonymous strangers. They too experience being alone and writing to a faceless someone, even though they have quite realistic images of who they are writing to. But the diary-keeping aspect of writing regular e-mail, combined with the emotional experience of introspection, enhances intimate communication even between established couples. For some couples, e-mail has actually enhanced or refreshed an existing relationship.

The most significant differences between e-mail romances in the workplace and those outside is that deception is more difficult and privacy is reduced or eliminated. All other aspects of Internet romances are possible in workplace relationships: obsession, fantasy, addiction and the seduction of the written word. For e-mail lovers in the workplace, my advice would be to conduct your e-mail relationship from home and don't use your work e-mail address—unless you own the company.

CHAPTER 9

Sorting It Out

If you have been involved in romances or in troubling relationships on the Internet, you may not know what to do or where—or even whether—to get help. But numerous resources for support and information are available, including (as a partial list) twelve-step programs, individual therapy and even support groups and chat rooms on the Internet itself. Search engines and your local yellow pages can help you find a wide range of self-help and treatment opportunities. Because so few resources are available, however, this chapter may help you sort out what is going on and what you can do about it.

Most of my psychotherapy patients are having some kind of problem with an Internet romance. They have told me:

1. **They are in love with someone they met on the Internet, and their marriage is suffering.**

2. **They are in love with someone who does not return the feeling.**

3. **They think they might be in love with someone they met on the Internet, but they aren't sure.**

4. **They have formed a pathological relationship with someone they met on the Internet.**

5. **They have become obsessed with or addicted to Internet communication.**

6. **They have become obsessed with or addicted to cybersex.**

7. **They have no life outside of their Internet activity.**

These problems may seem new because of the Internet connection, but they are actually much the same problems that people have always struggled with in relationships, transported into this new environment. The very newness of Internet-related problems often means that people do not feel comfortable talking about them in therapy (they don't want to look strange).

But Internet relationships do have unusual aspects that therapists may not be familiar with; it's important for therapists to find out about them. Just as with addiction to alcohol or cocaine, I have to ask my patients directly about their Internet use to find out that problems exist. As you try to understand your own Internet usage, you may wonder whether you are addicted, have a true obsession or a temporary fascination or just enjoy the creative aspects of Internet activity. Therapists may also wonder how to answer these questions.

When my patients find themselves in over their heads, I work with them to uncover their fantasies about their e-mail lovers. I also ask about the problems in their daily-life relationships that have led them to have an Internet affair. You can ask yourself some of these same questions.

INTERNET AFFAIRS

In the course of exploring the Internet, married people may find themselves involved in an intense and intimate relationship that eventually becomes threatening to their marriage. As John D. found, such a relationship can have an excitement and closeness that is not available in the marriage. Committed couples who would describe themselves as happy, let alone those who are struggling, have run up against the seduction of the easy intimacy of e-mail relationships.

If the marriage is to be saved, it is absolutely necessary that the Internet relationship be ended immediately. It is simply not possible to work on a marriage when most of one's energy, enthusiasm and excitement is being directed into an affair. Although some couples say an Internet affair spiced up their sex life or enhanced their ability to talk to each other, most affairs are destructive. If the goal is to improve the marriage or to save the relationship, the Internet affair must stop.

One of the first recommendations I would make to a married couple having this problem is to seek couples' counseling. But one partner may prefer to begin with individual therapy, in order to understand the importance of the online relationship. When Barbara came in to see me, her first question was "How could this be happening? I love my husband, he's my best friend. But I'm in love with a man I met online, and when I think about ending the relationship, I just fall apart." Barbara found herself obsessed with Gary, but when she tried to avoid answering his e-mail, she became irritated with her husband. Everything he did or said became annoying, and she began to wonder if she should divorce him.

In the course of therapy, it became apparent that Barbara's

husband wasn't annoying to her in a general sense, and that she still liked and loved him. But the excitement of the new relationship with Gary was more absorbing than her easy companionship with her husband. "It's like we don't have anything much to talk about anymore, and although I love him, I don't much feel like having sex. There's nothing particularly exciting about it, and I find myself thinking about Gary when I'm having sex with my husband."

Barbara had been married for twelve years, and before this computer relationship, she hadn't had any inclination to start an affair. Once or twice she had found herself attracted to a man at work, but she had always avoided further contact with those she found "too attractive." She met Gary accidentally in a discussion group about sex roles in the modern world, and he began to post private notes to her. After writing back and forth with Gary for about a month, Barbara began to feel that she was falling in love. She thought about him constantly and was eager to "talk" to him (to read and send e-mail). Her e-mails to him became lengthy; thinking about and writing them, and reading Gary's responses, absorbed much of her time.

When she didn't hear from Gary for a day, she would feel sad, and some days she would send as many as ten notes to him. They exchanged photographs, and her sexual fantasies were exclusively about him. Her heart skipped a beat whenever she found a note from him in her e-mail box, and soon they were talking on the phone. His voice excited and aroused her, but when she found herself actually planning a meeting with him, she decided that she needed therapy to deal with what had become a real problem for her.

As far as Barbara was concerned, she had fallen in love with Gary and now was faced with the dilemma of what to do about it. When I recommended that she seek couples' counseling with her husband, she was worried. "How will I tell him why I want to go to counseling? I haven't told him anything about what's going on, and he has no idea there are problems in the relationship. Until now, there haven't been any problems." But she agreed that her husband had noticed her increasing irritation with him and was wondering what was wrong.

Barbara finally did end the relationship with Gary, and she spent weeks feeling tearful and blue. She longed to talk to him and at times would find herself writing e-mail to him again; sometimes she sent them, and sometimes she deleted them without sending. The loss of her online relationship was as painful as the loss of any other relationship would be, and her grief led her again and again to want to reach out to Gary, just to make some contact.

It took Barbara about six months to stop feeling sad every time she thought of Gary. In individual therapy and in couples' counseling, some problems with the marriage came up— problems of which she had been unaware. Her belief that there were "no problems in the marriage" was not quite true, and yet had she not met Gary online, she probably wouldn't have gotten involved with another man. In the e-mail setting she was unable to judge her feelings or guard against the possibility of getting "too attracted" to someone, and she found herself "in love" before she knew what was happening.

By herself, Barbara was too scared of her husband's reaction to talk to him about her Internet romance. Only after months of couples' therapy did she finally begin to tell him about her experience. It was a rocky time for them both, but their marriage did survive.

Some couples do break up because of an Internet relationship. The new relationship can highlight a marriage problem, even emphasize it beyond the spouse's ability to tolerate it any further. A preexisting, chronic problem in a marriage can become a time bomb when a new relationship seems to offer a new way of life.

Andy told me that he had just been going through the motions of his marriage. He was depressed and unhappy with his life, so he immersed himself in work and didn't let himself think about it. Not until he started an intensely romantic relationship on the Internet did it become clear to him that he was deeply unhappy with his marriage. In the course of therapy, his dissatisfaction became almost intolerable, and he decided to end his ten-year marriage.

Andy wrote to me: "I felt happy for the first time in years. I hadn't known I was unhappy until I started to wake up in the morning looking forward to her e-mail, and I felt so good when there was a letter from her. The contrast was just too enormous. I couldn't stand the feeling of swinging back and forth from joy to depression—and I couldn't fix the marriage—actually, I didn't want to fix it. I needed to live again." He moved into his own apartment, but he never met his Internet lover in person; their relationship ended shortly afterward. For Andy, the affair itself wasn't as important as the marital problems that it brought to the surface. He later met another woman on the Internet who lived in a neighboring city; he says that this new relationship is going well and that "life feels worth living again."

Interestingly, many of the Internet affairs I heard about did not result in an actual face-to-face meeting, possibly due to geographic separation. All that happened was that one partner fell in love, and the couple experienced marriage and relationship problems because of someone neither of them had ever physically met. All the respondents reported that the excitement and secrecy of the relationship were just as significant as they imagined a real-life affair would be. Some of the marriages ended.

Affairs in ordinary life may not seem so prone to fantasy and projection, but fantasy does play a big part in any extramarital relationship, be it online or in person. The daily grind of house and children is absent from both kinds of affairs, and daydreams about a possible life together somehow never include fights about paying bills or dealing with in-laws.

A few established couples have worked on and improved their relationship via the Internet, exchanging e-mail and learning to communicate with each other in some of the same intimate ways they talk with strangers. It's not as easy for such couples to be intimate with each other, but it is sometimes more possible when they are not in the same room reacting to what each other is saying. The introspective nature of writing, and taking time to think about their replies to each other's letters, can bring a married couple closer together.

One couple did report that cybersex added new heat to their own failing sexual relationship, but I don't think I would recommend that to most people. But couples whose sexual interest in each other is flagging need to pay attention to the problem and look for ways within the marriage to spark some novelty and enjoyment. Self-help books are readily available to help put the joy back into your sex life, and some therapists specialize in the treatment of sexual problems in marriage. But any couple should always be aware of potential problems so that they can work on them together, before a more dangerous "solution" sends one partner an e-mail.

IS IT REAL LOVE?

In both real-life and e-mail relationships, the question of whether a feeling constitutes "real love" arises reasonably frequently in therapy. The feelings associated with falling in love are difficult to quantify, yet our culture attaches tremendous importance to being "truly in love" as a basis for further relationships.

For some people, the question of real love is complicated by the relative novelty of computer communication. The idea that you could fall in love, in real love, with a stranger you know only through e-mail is confusing and upsetting. One of the reasons I began working with the subject of Internet romance is that very confusion. How real can an experience be if it is based on an "unreal" interaction?

The second question after "Is it real love?" should be "Is this a good idea?" Therapists have been dealing with this question about 3-D relationships for years; the twists of the Internet add some factors that should be explored. As you discuss your relationship with your online lover, it's important to understand the degree of fantasy and idealization involved in online communication. The question of meeting the online lover and the problems associated with conducting any relationship long distance all can complicate an online romance. And as I mentioned before, the possibility that your lover is being deceptive is much greater in an Internet romance.

PATHOLOGICAL RELATIONSHIPS

Second only to major psychiatric illnesses, pathological or dysfunctional relationships plague many e-mail lovers.

Although anyone can find themselves in a disturbed relationship in ordinary life, the Internet seems to open the door for troubled love affairs.

Pathological relationships online differ from those that happen face to face primarily in the areas of fantasy, obsession and deception. Since online romances are so laden with opportunities for fantasy, the conflicts between fantasy and reality are even more common than in ordinary-life relationships.

The obsessive quality of love in general, combined with the obsessive quality of computer relationships, can produce a preoccupation with an online lover that is greater than it would be in an ordinary relationship. The possibility of virtually continual contact with the person can enhance your emotional dependence, even to the point that you become "addicted" to the other person.

As we have seen, deception can run rampant in computer relationships. You may even have brought some deception into the relationship yourself. Relationships get distorted when even misrepresentations are made. Your own family history, your previous problems with relationships and your honesty about them all will color your computer relationship. A dysfunctional relationship with an e-mail lover can simply replay problems you have had in relationships in daily life.

I have already talked about some of the ways to explore deception in e-mail relationships. Only you can decide how much deception is damaging and how much is just ordinary human behavior. Is it important that he said he is five foot ten inches tall when he really is only five foot eight? Or that she says she's a few pounds overweight, when it's actually twenty-five pounds? A mild enhancement of one's physical self-description is probably not as problematic as a deception about previous relationships, the existence of children or employment status. If your lover neglects to mention that he lives with his parents, or that she hasn't quite completed her divorce proceedings, this relationship is clearly not a good idea, no matter how intensely you are in love.

The degree to which you idealize your Internet relationship is the degree to which you will later be disappointed and even angry. If you meet someone with no flaws, Mr. or Ms. Wonderful, you have probably idealized them. You need to explore the real aspects of your lover that amount to serious drawbacks—the ones that are meaningful to you—as honestly as you can. Get a friend to help you sort out the person's flaws and any reservations that you may have. If he is a fishing fanatic, while your idea of camping is staying at a Motel 6 instead of the Hilton, that is a real drawback. If she is much older or much younger than you are completely comfortable with, then you need to at least talk about your reservations about the relationship. Remember that someone who is verbal, articulate and funny on the Internet may be anxious and shy in person.

If you can't think of any drawbacks or flaws or reservations, then either you are not being honest or you haven't found out enough about each other. No one is flawless. It's a lot easier to miss a person's ordinary flaws on the Internet than in person. The existence of flaws doesn't in itself mean the relationship isn't good; it just means you need to be aware and honest with yourself about how important they are. A frank and honest discussion of your concerns about the relationship with your online beloved can actually enhance intimacy, and enhance the likelihood that your relationship will be worthwhile and durable.

INTERNET ADDICTION

Although an Internet addiction may not cost as much as an addiction to cocaine or gambling, it can be expensive to the point of costing hundreds of dollars a month. In terms of destroying your life, it can be just as severe as any other addiction.

In 1993 a young man in England was acquitted of computer hacking charges after his defense team argued that he was an Internet addict.[1] According to his mother, "he had few friends, spent most of his time computing and frequently forgot to eat and sleep when he was hacking online." Faced with huge phone bills, she asked British Teleco to secure her line with a password of four digits. But he got around even this difficulty when he "got his computer to monitor the line, record her keystrokes, then play them back when he wanted to dial out."

If you suspect you have an Internet addiction, you should ask yourself the following questions.[2] They are similar to the criteria for substance addiction as developed by Ivan Goldberg based on the *Diagnostic and Statistical Manual of Mental Disorders,* with specific questions designed to assess Internet addiction.

Over the past one-year period, have you found that:

1. **You think about the Internet while offline.**

2. **You have an increasing need to use the Internet to achieve satisfaction.**

3. **You're unable to control your Internet use.**

4. **You feel restless or irritable when attempting to cut down or stop Internet use.**

5. **You use the Internet as a way of escaping from problems or relieving a poor mood.**

6. **You lie to family members or friends to conceal the extent of your Internet involvement.**

7. **You are jeopardizing a significant relationship, job or educational or career opportunity because of your Internet use.**

8. **You keep returning even after spending an excessive amount of money on online fees.**

9. **You go through "withdrawal" when offline.**

10. **You regularly stay online longer than you intended.**

If four or more of these statements apply to you, then you most likely have an Internet addiction. You need to get treatment for it, as you would for any other addiction, either through a twelve-step program based on the Alcoholics Anonymous format, or through individual therapy.

Twelve-step programs can be as useful in treating an Internet addiction as in treating any other addiction. Support groups are available online, which may be the first step toward recovery in spite of the location. If no Internet addiction group is available in the person's neighborhood, an Alcoholics Anonymous, Narcotics Anonymous, Gamblers Anonymous or Overeaters Anonymous group may be helpful to those who find themselves unable to stop their excessive Internet use.

I recommend to my Internet-addicted patients that they find a sponsor in Alcoholics Anonymous or in Overeaters Anonymous who understands the addictive nature of the Internet. I also recommend that they attend twelve-step meetings—and get out of the house, away from the computer. As with alcoholics and narcotics addicts, I generally recommend that they attend "thirty meetings in thirty days" as an initial step—that is, that they attend one meeting of an addiction group every day for a month.

It is hard for many people to substitute the word *Internet* for the word *alcohol* as they go through a twelve-step program; nonetheless, I encourage them to participate because it has been helpful for many—once they are able to make the substitution. Individual therapy is an important adjunct to a twelve-step program because many or even most of the Internet addicts have underlying problems that make them vulnerable to Internet abuse—problems that could just as easily lead them to other destructive addictions.

Unlike alcoholism or cocaine addicts, many Internet addicts are unable to completely avoid using the substance they abuse because they must use the Internet for research or e-mail related to their work. Like people with eating disorders, Internet addicts usually cannot stop "cold turkey" as a way of treating their addiction. That is one reason Overeaters Anonymous is a good resource for Internet addicts, because it deals with the same kinds of day-to-day problems.

Depression that comes from terminating an Internet connection should be treated with therapy and even, if it's severe, with antidepressant medication. Anxiety and "withdrawal" symptoms can be treated with relaxation techniques, self-hypnosis or calling one's sponsor, or in some cases with acupuncture or an antianxiety medication.

INTERNET OBSESSION

Another approach to alleviating an Internet problem is to look at it as an "obsession" rather than as an addiction. I'm using the word *obsession* here in the common definition, not in the formal psychiatric definition. People who become obsessed with the Internet are preoccupied to the point of being uninterested in anything else. Like an addiction, an obsession can fill your life, but it doesn't operate exactly as an addiction does. You don't need higher and higher doses to get satisfaction, and lying about your usage doesn't usually arise with an obsession. In fact, most of the people I know who are obsessed with the Internet tend to brag about the amount of time they spend online. Although some severely obsessed people may seem like addicts, most obsessed people are not jeopardizing their job, their relationships or their finances with their preoccupation.

One mode of treatment for obsession is psychotherapy. The primary focus of therapy is to treat the underlying problem, which in some cases is a true obsessive-compulsive disorder. One of my patients felt compelled to work on her e-mail responses, rewriting them again and again until she had them "perfect." If she sent one out without rewriting, she became extremely anxious and had a feeling that something terrible was going to happen. She had this kind of difficulty with many activities, doing them over and over again until they were perfect; the Internet was only one of her areas of concern.

Some twenty years ago, when Dungeons and Dragons was popular, many young people spent hours and whole days working on their game roles and even constructed costumes and wrote lengthy descriptions of their characters. Some of my friends played these games for days, going without sleep and sometimes without food (due to budgetary concerns) while the game went on. Their college work suffered, and several were forced to withdraw from school because of failing grades. They were obsessed with the game, focusing on it to the exclusion of all other activities.

In retrospect, it is clear to me that they were not addicted to the game as much as they were fascinated or obsessed with it. They were obsessed with its role-playing, its intricacies and its social aspects. The multi-user dungeons (MUDs) and chat boards available throughout the Internet today can also create this kind of fascination—because they *are* interesting, and because for many participants, they provide a degree of social interaction and role-playing that is just not available in every-day life.

The fascination with creativity must be understood as you wonder if you are obsessed with the Internet. Anyone who has ever had experience with an artist or writer knows that obses-sion is an essential component of their work, and attempts to change that obsession can be met with resistance or outright rejection. Even when an artist is seeking a more balanced life, the fascination with the work can overwhelm his best attempts to stop working in time for dinner with the family, or to go to bed when his wife is going to bed.

Role-playing, writing and reading e-mail on a variety of subjects, "talking" to friends until the wee hours of the morn-ing—all these are fascinating and interesting activities that are more similar to creative activity than to other pastimes. Games happen in real time, as do chat rooms and private con-versations on the Internet. They can go on until the partici-pants collapse from exhaustion, then continue long after that as new participants come online and join in.

As I have already noted, even friendly e-mail has a deeply introspective quality. In a working life, you may have few other opportunities to spend time with yourself; to explore exactly how you feel about your new boss, about some recent bomb-ing, about the new tax bill or about having or not having chil-dren. You may want and need to use the Internet for this kind of introspection without becoming obsessed or addicted. If you have any doubt, ask yourself whether it has pushed other normal interests out of your life. If your answer is no, most likely you don't have an addiction.

During times of trouble or change, some people temporarily become preoccupied with their Internet activities and use e-mail correspondence to explore the changes they are facing. A midlife crisis may draw a middle-aged person to the Internet, just as a student who is away at college or a married person who is feeling alone after a separation may find the Internet to be the most important aspect of daily life—for a while.

Many of these ordinary "obsessions," in my observation, run a course of three to six months of intense Internet activity, after which, for most people, the activity loses its fascination. Cybersex gets boring, or the chat room begins to seem repetitive. Those involved in role-playing games drop out for periods of time or construct new characters. For some people, the Internet obsession turns into a life's work—from playing with the computer, they move on to working with the computer.

CYBERSEX

The possibility of having "sex" with multiple partners many times in a single session is very attractive to some people. And developing an "addiction" to cybersex is certainly a possibility. In ordinary life, some people develop a true psychological addiction to sexual activity. Sex Addicts Anonymous was formed for the purpose of helping them.

Not everyone who engages in cybersex becomes addicted, and for those who have no symptoms of addiction, regularly engaging in cybersex is not an illness.

For most participants, the sexual exploration of new sexual ideas and sexual activities is an important facet of cybersex. Its excitement and novelty stem at least partly from this exploration, while the novelty of simply participating in computer sex with strangers is arousing for many who exchange sexual fantasies online. For someone who has a long-standing relationship, this novelty effect can either increase their sexual enjoyment with their partner or increase their dissatisfaction; and where dissatisfaction becomes a problem, cybersex can widen the rift and permanently damage the relationship.

The movement from enjoying novelty in sexual experiences to *requiring* it can increase sexual activity via the Internet to the point that face-to-face relationships are no longer adequately stimulating. The Internet makes access to novel sexual activity easy for many people—they don't have to worry about being seen coming out of an adult bookstore or getting arrested in a sex-shop raid. Access to novel sexual experiences can be immediate, while few real-life relationships operate that way.

Like a physical affair, cybersex can severely impede your sexual interest in your husband or wife. If you are in this situation, and you want to work toward saving your relationship, your online activity *must be discontinued.*

I recommend Sex Addicts Anonymous and psychotherapy for those who are obsessed with or addicted to cybersex.

"I HAVE NO LIFE."

As we have seen, some people have no life outside their Internet activity. They may be agoraphobic, they may work at home or they may simply never leave the house without a companion. Some are very anxious and uncomfortable in social situations and literally have no friends in the 3-D world. All of their social activity comes from Internet connections and chat boards.

Others are brought into treatment by their family members because they are terribly isolated, spending all their time on the computer. They themselves usually do not feel they have a problem—they are quite content to spend all their time alone, engaged in projects on the computer. Interestingly, people who prefer being alone are not particularly engaged on the chat boards—they don't need the companionship. Sometimes they are involved in role-playing games, but even on the Internet, most of their activities are solitary.

For seriously shy or truly social phobic people, meeting others in person can be a nightmare. Most of us have had the experience of making a serious *faux pas* in public and vividly remember the feeling of excruciating embarrassment or shame associated with that experience. For seriously shy people, every social contact carries that degree of discomfort. Understandably, they would prefer not to have it. It is a kind of social anxiety, or if it is really severe, it's a social phobia. Being alone at home, safe and anonymous on the computer, may be the only comfortable social contact that such people can have.

But for those who long for real companionship or a face-to-face social world, the computer is ultimately unsatisfying. Computer friends are not the same as real friends, people to go shopping with or out to a ballgame. A computer doesn't replace traveling, dancing or dating. Still, I do *not* recommend that isolated people discontinue their Internet connections. It would be unreasonable to deprive them of the only remotely satisfying social contact they have on a regular basis. In fact, some people simply may never reach the level of social comfort necessary to join a club or church, or to date successfully.

In dealing with this social anxiety, you may find relaxation techniques and psychotherapy useful. Some people may do well in group therapy, where they can practice relating to people face to face. Recovery Inc., a self-help program for people with anxiety problems, can be a very helpful—and inexpensive— resource for those who have anxiety in many situations.

If you think you have a true social phobia, you may benefit from taking an antidepressant medication. If you are disabled by your social anxiety, I would strongly recommend that you consider talking to your doctor about such a medication.

Many very useful forums and Usenet groups on the Internet devote themselves to depression, antidepressant medications, anxiety problems and a host of other psychological and psychiatric difficulties. Since the addresses change so rapidly, I would suggest using an Internet search engine to track them down.

THE INTERNET CAN BE HELPFUL

Some people suffering from depression have found these Internet groups and relationships to be supportive and interesting, even to have a therapeutic effect. The self-exploration that is made possible through writing e-mail, the connection with other live humans at any time of the day or night and the emotional support available through Usenet groups—all can be helpful for those struggling with depression.

I also recommend that my patients explore the Internet for information about medications, support groups for particular illnesses and even for companionship at odd hours when others in their life are unavailable. One group of chat-board participants responded to a suicide threat by keeping the person online while others researched where the person was and notified authorities about the danger. In other cases, information on medical treatment for a childhood illness that a parent found on a chat board devoted to parenting issues saved their child's life by making possible an appropriate referral.

Considering that many if not most Internet groups are not hosted by professionals, I would suggest that you be somewhat wary about the advice you get from them. The advice you get may be not only conflicting but occasionally dead wrong. If you are researching medication, be sure to look at the formal medical information available through such sources as Grateful Med, before you engage in a freewheeling discussion with other people about their varied experiences. If you are participating in a chat group, consult more authoritative sources before you follow your computer friends' advice.

Although you should take some care to avoid developing an excessive dependence on the Internet, I believe that for the majority of people the possible benefits of Internet activity outweigh the dangers. And for those who are seeking a romantic companion, the Internet offers many opportunities to make emotional connections outside of those that hitherto have been available.

Finally, I also offer my patients the opportunity to contact me via my own e-mail address. This provides a forum for discussing medication side effects and making a connection with me without disturbing me or interrupting me. The e-mail opportunity is available even when I am out of town or otherwise unavailable (like when I'm sleeping!). E-mail contact with my patients is beneficial to me as well, since I can print out messages to become part of the patient's permanent file and can respond with directions that will not be garbled as they could be with phone messages or messages left with family members. And then I can print out my instructions for future reference.

Although the Internet is new, most of the issues I've discussed in this book are not new at all. When I told people what I was writing about, they often said to me, "Wow! That's really new stuff, isn't it?" But people have been meeting and falling in love in unusual ways ever since human beings first began to fall in love at all. From arranged marriages to letters to "any soldier," and from asking "What's your sign?" in a bar to asking "What's your operating system?" on CompuServe, falling in love holds an ancient fascination. All that new technology has given us is new ways to experience the same old human delights and failings.

As the saying goes, new solutions do breed new problems. The Internet provides a few new problems, including the opportunity for people to meet without information about their physical appearance. This opportunity is creating some new human experiences that we don't yet have rules to deal with. Instantaneous communication, access to whole new worlds of experience, exposure to people we would not meet in ordinary life—we haven't figured out what the outcome will be. But it is clear that people will continue to fall in love via the Internet. I hope this book has helped you understand how it can happen that an ordinary person, even someone you know, can fall in love with a stranger online.

If you were wondering what happened in the relationships I have described, here is a brief follow-up on some of them (even composites have a happily-ever-after!):

Cadet and Circe finally met after six months of their computer romance. Cadet moved to Australia, where he is now working as a nurse. They have been married for five months.

John D. (Warrior8) and Starchild met and had a brief affair. John found that he didn't want to leave his wife, and he and Paula are now in therapy to work on their marriage. Starchild has met another man on the Internet and hopes he will be "the one."

Wendy and Karl never did meet. They have continued to write, but their finances make it impossible to get together, so currently they write only occasionally. Wendy is dating a man she met through a singles' group, and Karl is having another Internet relationship.

HooperD and AbleSusan are still married, and aside from the problems AbleSusan is having with Immigration and Naturalization, they say they are doing well.

Stallion and Lady Peace are living in the same city now and are considering moving in together. They have some problems they hadn't foreseen, including Stallion's ongoing career problems. They still write notes on the Internet, but their previous rapid-fire correspondence has been replaced by dating in person.

Claire gave up computer activity entirely. She had her husband pull the modem out of the computer and delete all the programs that access the Internet. She is now participating in an Overeaters Anonymous group, though she tells me that it is sometimes hard to make her friends there understand that her computer addiction is really that serious a problem.

Jonathan was unable to continue his computer relationship. His girlfriend wanted to meet him, but he couldn't bring himself to face her with the level of deception he felt he had brought to their relationship. He has vowed to make sure to be honest in his next relationship.

Sam and Mary have been planning their wedding, and their co-workers are buying them a new modem as a wedding gift (which they will know by the time this book comes to press <g>).

Susan and Harry dated for about three months, then drifted apart. Harry is now dating another woman he met on the Internet who lives in his same city.

Sophia and Joseph have found new jobs, but their own relationship went sour in the wake of the upset and anger around Joseph getting fired. They no longer write to each other at all.

Carla and Sam have been married for about four years now, and they tell me things are going well, with a baby on the way.

Barbara and her husband divorced after another two years of troubles in their marriage. Barbara swears she will stay away from the Internet—she feels that the marriage never really recovered from the blow of her Internet affair.

ENDNOTES

PREFACE

1. W. H. Weiss, "Getting Connected Electronically: The Internet," *National Research Bureau,* vol. 57 (Jan. 1, 1996).

CHAPTER 2: THE INTIMACY OF ONLINE COMMUNICATION

1. Joanne, "Offline Meetings," downloaded from the Internet, date unknown.

2. Gary Chapman, "Flamers," *New Republic,* vol. 212 (Apr. 10, 1995).

CHAPTER 3: IN LOVE BEFORE YOU KNOW IT

1. Joanne, "Offline Meetings," downloaded from Internet, date unknown.

CHAPTER 4: IS IT *REAL* LOVE?

1. Bernard Murstein, "A Taxonomy of Love," in Robert J. Sternberg and Michael L. Barnes, eds., *The Psychology of Love* (New Haven: Yale University Press, 1988).

2. Robert J. Sternberg, "Triangulating Love," in Robert J. Sternberg and Michael L. Barnes, eds., *The Psychology of Love* (New Haven: Yale University Press, 1988).

3. Avodah Offit, "Are You Ready for Virtual Love? A Psychiatrist Looks at Cybersex," *Cosmopolitan,* vol. 218 (Jan. 1995).

CHAPTER 5: ELECTRONIC ADULTERY

1. Sue Shellenbarger, "Growing Web Use Alters the Dynamics of Life at Home," *Wall Street Journal,* Nov. 20, 1996.

2. Ibid.

3. Stephanie Fletcher, *E-mail, A Love Story* (Donald I. Fine Books, 1996).

4. Robert Sternberg, "Triangulating Love," in Robert J. Sternberg and Michael L. Barnes, eds., *The Psychology of Love* (New Haven: Yale University Press, 1988); and W. H. Weiss, "Getting Connected Electronically: The Internet," *National Research Bureau*, vol. 57 (Jan. 1, 1996).

CHAPTER 6: OBSESSION AND ADDICTION

1. Shari Roan, "Can't Get Enough of the Net?" *Los Angeles Times*, Aug. 13, 1996.

2. Katherine Maurer, "Internet 'Addiction' Surfs into Therapists' Offices," *Clinical Psychiatry News*, vol. 24, no. 10 (Oct. 1996).

3. Kendall Hamilton and Claudia Kalb, "They Log On, But They Can't Log Off," *Newsweek*, Dec. 18, 1995.

4. "Internet Can Be Addictive," *National Psychologist*, Sept./Oct. 1996.

5. Sherry Turkle, *Life on the Screen: Identity in the Age of the Internet* (New York: Simon & Schuster, 1995).

CHAPTER 7: PATHOLOGICAL RELATIONSHIPS

1. John Sullivan, "Others Tell of E-Mailing Suspect in Torture Case," *New York Times*, Dec. 10, 1996.

2. Jesse Kornbluth, "First Person: You Make Me Feel Like a . . . Virtual Woman," *Los Angeles Times*, Jan. 6, 1995.

3. "Online Words May Haunt You," *Orlando Sentinel*, Mar. 10, 1996.

4. Elizabeth Snead, "Fanatic Attraction: Increasingly, Stalkers Make Fame a Risky Proposition," *USA Today*, Aug. 29, 1996.

5. Susan Malestic, "When Love Becomes Obsession," *Single Parent*, June 1, 1994.

6. Jessica Kowal, "Terror in Cyberspace," *Newsday*, Nov. 16, 1995.

CHAPTER 8: WORK AND LOVE

1. Leslie Helm, "The Digital Smoking Gun," *Los Angeles Times*, June 16, 1994.

2. Martha Groves, "Work Force Diversity: An Affinity for E-mail," *Los Angeles Times*, May 16, 1994.

CHAPTER 9: SORTING IT OUT

1. Ian McClelland, "Computers in the '90s: Confessions of the Online Junkie," *Newsday,* June 27, 1995.

2. Shari Roan, "Can't Get Enough of the Net?" *Los Angeles Times,* Aug. 13, 1996; and *Diagnostic and Statistical Manual of Mental Disorders,* 4th ed. (American Psychiatric Association, 1994).